TABLE OF CONTENTS

The Law School Admission Test is a half-day standardized test required for admission to all ABA-approved law schools, most Canadian law schools, and many other law schools. It consists of five 35-minute sections of multiple-choice questions. Four of the five sections contribute to the test taker's score. These sections include one reading comprehension section, one analytical reasoning section, and two logical reasoning sections. The unscored section, commonly referred to as the variable section, typically is used to pretest new test questions or to preequate new test forms. The placement of this section in the LSAT will vary. A 35-minute writing sample is administered at the end of the test. The writing sample is not scored by LSAC, but copies are sent to all law schools to which you apply. The score scale for the LSAT is 120 to 180.

The LSAT is designed to measure skills considered essential for success in law school: the reading and comprehension of complex texts with accuracy and insight; the organization and management of information and the ability to draw reasonable inferences from it; the ability to think critically; and the analysis and evaluation of the reasoning and arguments of others.

The LSAT provides a standard measure of acquired reading and verbal reasoning skills that law schools can use as one of several factors in assessing applicants.

For up-to-date information about LSAC's services, go to our website, LSAC.org.

SCORING

Your LSAT score is based on the number of questions you answer correctly (the raw score). There is no deduction for incorrect answers, and all questions count equally. In other words, there is no penalty for guessing.

Test Score Accuracy—Reliability and Standard Error of Measurement

Candidates perform at different levels on different occasions for reasons quite unrelated to the characteristics of a test itself. The accuracy of test scores is best described by the use of two related statistical terms: reliability and standard error of measurement.

Reliability is a measure of how consistently a test measures the skills being assessed. The higher the reliability coefficient for a test, the more certain we can be that test takers would get very similar scores if they took the test again.

LSAC reports an internal consistency measure of reliability for every test form. Reliability can vary from 0.00 to 1.00, and a test with no measurement error would have a reliability coefficient of 1.00 (never attained in practice). Reliability

coefficients for past LSAT forms have ranged from .90 to .95, indicating a high degree of consistency for these tests. LSAC expects the reliability of the LSAT to continue to fall within the same range.

LSAC also reports the amount of measurement error associated with each test form, a concept known as the standard error of measurement (SEM). The SEM, which is usually about 2.6 points, indicates how close a test taker's observed score is likely to be to his or her true score. True scores are theoretical scores that would be obtained from perfectly reliable tests with no measurement error—scores never known in practice.

Score bands, or ranges of scores that contain a test taker's true score a certain percentage of the time, can be derived using the SEM. LSAT score bands are constructed by adding and subtracting the (rounded) SEM to and from an actual LSAT score (e.g., the LSAT score, plus or minus 3 points). Scores near 120 or 180 have asymmetrical bands. Score bands constructed in this manner will contain an individual's true score approximately 68 percent of the time.

Measurement error also must be taken into account when comparing LSAT scores of two test takers. It is likely that small differences in scores are due to measurement error rather than to meaningful differences in ability. The standard error of score differences provides some guidance as to the importance of differences between two scores. The standard error of score differences is approximately 1.4 times larger than the standard error of measurement for the individual scores.

Thus, a test score should be regarded as a useful but approximate measure of a test taker's abilities as measured by the test, not as an exact determination of his or her abilities. LSAC encourages law schools to examine the range of scores within the interval that probably contains the test taker's true score (e.g., the test taker's score band) rather than solely interpret the reported score alone.

Adjustments for Variation in Test Difficulty

All test forms of the LSAT reported on the same score scale are designed to measure the same abilities, but one test form may be slightly easier or more difficult than another. The scores from different test forms are made comparable through a statistical procedure known as equating. As a result of equating, a given scaled score earned on different test forms reflects the same level of ability.

Research on the LSAT

Summaries of LSAT validity studies and other LSAT research can be found in member law school libraries and at LSAC.org.

To Inquire About Test Questions

If you find what you believe to be an error or ambiguity in a test question that affects your response to the question, contact LSAC by e-mail: *LSATTS@LSAC.org*, or write to Law School Admission Council, Test Development Group, Box 40, Newtown, PA 18940-0040.

HOW THIS PREPTEST DIFFERS FROM AN ACTUAL LSAT

This PrepTest is made up of the scored sections and writing sample from the actual disclosed LSAT administered in June 2010. However, it does not contain the extra, variable section that is used to pretest new test items of one of the three multiple-choice question types. The three multiple-choice question types may be in a different order in an actual LSAT than in this PrepTest. This is because the order of these question types is intentionally varied for each administration of the test.

THE THREE LSAT MULTIPLE-CHOICE QUESTION TYPES

The multiple-choice questions that make up most of the LSAT reflect a broad range of academic disciplines and are intended to give no advantage to candidates from a particular academic background.

The five sections of the test contain three different question types. The following material presents a general discussion of the nature of each question type and some strategies that can be used in answering them.

Analytical Reasoning Questions

Analytical Reasoning questions are designed to assess the ability to consider a group of facts and rules, and, given those facts and rules, determine what could or must be true. The specific scenarios associated with these questions are usually unrelated to law, since they are intended to be accessible to a wide range of test takers. However, the skills tested parallel those involved in determining what could or must be the case given a set of regulations, the terms of a contract, or the facts of a legal case in relation to the law. In Analytical Reasoning questions, you are asked to reason deductively from a set of statements and rules or principles that describe relationships among persons, things, or events.

Analytical Reasoning questions appear in sets, with each set based on a single passage. The passage used for each set of questions describes common ordering relationships or grouping relationships, or a combination of both types of relationships. Examples include scheduling employees for work shifts, assigning instructors to class sections,

ordering tasks according to priority, and distributing grants for projects.

Analytical Reasoning questions test a range of deductive reasoning skills. These include:

- Comprehending the basic structure of a set of relationships by determining a complete solution to the problem posed (for example, an acceptable seating arrangement of all six diplomats around a table)

- Reasoning with conditional ("if-then") statements and recognizing logically equivalent formulations of such statements

- Inferring what could be true or must be true from given facts and rules

- Inferring what could be true or must be true from given facts and rules together with new information in the form of an additional or substitute fact or rule

- Recognizing when two statements are logically equivalent in context by identifying a condition or rule that could replace one of the original conditions while still resulting in the same possible outcomes

Analytical Reasoning questions reflect the kinds of detailed analyses of relationships and sets of constraints that a law student must perform in legal problem solving. For example, an Analytical Reasoning passage might describe six diplomats being seated around a table, following certain rules of protocol as to who can sit where. You, the test taker, must answer questions about the logical implications of given and new information. For example, you may be asked who can sit between diplomats X and Y, or who cannot sit next to X if W sits next to Y. Similarly, if you were a student in law school, you might be asked to analyze a scenario involving a set of particular circumstances and a set of governing rules in the form of constitutional provisions, statutes, administrative codes, or prior rulings that have been upheld. You might then be asked to determine the legal options in the scenario: what is required given the scenario, what is permissible given the scenario, and what is prohibited given the scenario. Or you might be asked to develop a "theory" for the case: when faced with an incomplete set of facts about the case, you must fill in the picture based on what is implied by the facts that are known. The problem could be elaborated by the addition of new information or hypotheticals.

No formal training in logic is required to answer these questions correctly. Analytical Reasoning questions are intended to be answered using knowledge, skills, and reasoning ability generally expected of college students and graduates.

Suggested Approach

Some people may prefer to answer first those questions about a passage that seem less difficult and then those that seem more difficult. In general, it is best to finish one passage before starting on another, because much time can be lost in returning to a passage and reestablishing familiarity with its relationships. However, if you are having great difficulty on one particular set of questions and are spending too much time on them, it may be to your advantage to skip that set of questions and go on to the next passage, returning to the problematic set of questions after you have finished the other questions in the section.

Do not assume that because the conditions for a set of questions look long or complicated, the questions based on those conditions will be especially difficult.

Read the passage carefully. Careful reading and analysis are necessary to determine the exact nature of the relationships involved in an Analytical Reasoning passage. Some relationships are fixed (for example, P and R must always work on the same project). Other relationships are variable (for example, Q must be assigned to either team 1 or team 3). Some relationships that are not stated explicitly in the conditions are implied by and can be deduced from those that are stated (for example, if one condition about paintings in a display specifies that Painting K must be to the left of Painting Y, and another specifies that Painting W must be to the left of Painting K, then it can be deduced that Painting W must be to the left of Painting Y).

In reading the conditions, do not introduce unwarranted assumptions. For instance, in a set of questions establishing relationships of height and weight among the members of a team, do not assume that a person who is taller than another person must weigh more than that person. As another example, suppose a set involves ordering and a question in the set asks what must be true if both X and Y must be earlier than Z; in this case, do not assume that X must be earlier than Y merely because X is mentioned before Y. All the information needed to answer each question is provided in the passage and the question itself.

The conditions are designed to be as clear as possible. Do not interpret the conditions as if they were intended to trick you. For example, if a question asks how many people could be eligible to serve on a committee, consider only those people named in the passage unless directed otherwise. When in doubt, read the conditions in their most obvious sense. Remember, however, that the language in the conditions is intended to be read for precise meaning. It is essential to pay particular attention to words that describe or limit relationships, such as "only," "exactly," "never," "always," "must be," "cannot be," and the like.

The result of this careful reading will be a clear picture of the structure of the relationships involved, including the kinds of relationships permitted, the participants in the relationships, and the range of possible actions or attributes for these participants.

Keep in mind question independence. Each question should be considered separately from the other questions in its set. No information, except what is given in the original conditions, should be carried over from one question to another.

In some cases a question will simply ask for conclusions to be drawn from the conditions as originally given. Some questions may, however, add information to the original conditions or temporarily suspend or replace one of the original conditions for the purpose of that question only. For example, if Question 1 adds the supposition "if P is sitting at table 2 ...," this supposition should NOT be carried over to any other question in the set.

Consider highlighting text and using diagrams. Many people find it useful to underline key points in the passage and in each question. In addition, it may prove very helpful to draw a diagram to assist you in finding the solution to the problem.

In preparing for the test, you may wish to experiment with different types of diagrams. For a scheduling problem, a simple calendar-like diagram may be helpful. For a grouping problem, an array of labeled columns or rows may be useful.

Even though most people find diagrams to be very helpful, some people seldom use them, and for some individual questions no one will need a diagram. There is by no means universal agreement on which kind of diagram is best for which problem or in which cases a diagram is most useful. Do not be concerned if a particular problem in the test seems to be best approached without the use of a diagram.

Logical Reasoning Questions

Arguments are a fundamental part of the law, and analyzing arguments is a key element of legal analysis. Training in the law builds on a foundation of basic reasoning skills. Law students must draw on the skills of analyzing, evaluating, constructing, and refuting arguments. They need to be able to identify what information is relevant to an issue or argument and what impact further evidence might have. They need to be able to reconcile opposing positions and use arguments to persuade others.

Logical Reasoning questions evaluate the ability to analyze, critically evaluate, and complete arguments as they occur in ordinary language. The questions are based on short arguments drawn from a wide variety of sources, including newspapers, general interest magazines, scholarly publications, advertisements, and informal discourse. These arguments mirror legal reasoning in the types of arguments presented and in their complexity, though few of the arguments actually have law as a subject matter.

Each Logical Reasoning question requires you to read and comprehend a short passage, then answer one question (or, rarely, two questions) about it. The questions are designed to assess a wide range of skills involved in thinking critically, with an emphasis on skills that are central to legal reasoning.

These skills include:

- Recognizing the parts of an argument and their relationships

- Recognizing similarities and differences between patterns of reasoning

- Drawing well-supported conclusions

- Reasoning by analogy

- Recognizing misunderstandings or points of disagreement

- Determining how additional evidence affects an argument

- Detecting assumptions made by particular arguments

- Identifying and applying principles or rules

- Identifying flaws in arguments

- Identifying explanations

The questions do not presuppose specialized knowledge of logical terminology. For example, you will not be expected to know the meaning of specialized terms such as "ad hominem" or "syllogism." On the other hand, you will be expected to understand and critique the reasoning contained in arguments. This requires that you possess a university-level understanding of widely used concepts such as argument, premise, assumption, and conclusion.

Suggested Approach

Read each question carefully. Make sure that you understand the meaning of each part of the question. Make sure that you understand the meaning of each answer choice and the ways in which it may or may not relate to the question posed.

Do not pick a response simply because it is a true statement. Although true, it may not answer the question posed.

Answer each question on the basis of the information that is given, even if you do not agree with it. Work within the context provided by the passage. LSAT questions do not involve any tricks or hidden meanings.

Reading Comprehension Questions

Both law school and the practice of law revolve around extensive reading of highly varied, dense, argumentative and expository texts (for example, cases, codes, contracts, briefs, decisions, evidence). This reading must be exacting, distinguishing precisely what is said from what is not said. It involves comparison, analysis, synthesis, and application (for example, of principles and rules). It involves drawing appropriate inferences and applying ideas and arguments to new contexts. Law school reading also requires the ability to grasp unfamiliar subject matter and the ability to penetrate difficult and challenging material.

The purpose of LSAT Reading Comprehension questions is to measure the ability to read, with understanding and insight, examples of lengthy and complex materials similar to those commonly encountered in law school. The Reading Comprehension section of the LSAT contains four sets of reading questions, each set consisting of a selection of reading material followed by five to eight questions. The reading selection in three of the four sets consists of a single reading passage; the other set contains two related shorter passages. Sets with two passages are a variant of Reading Comprehension called Comparative Reading, which was introduced in June 2007.

Comparative Reading questions concern the relationships between the two passages, such as those of generalization/instance, principle/application, or point/counterpoint. Law school work often requires reading two or more texts in conjunction with each other and understanding their relationships. For example, a law student may read a trial court decision together with an appellate court decision that overturns it, or identify the fact pattern from a hypothetical suit together with the potentially controlling case law.

Reading selections for LSAT Reading Comprehension questions are drawn from a wide range of subjects in the humanities, the social sciences, the biological and physical sciences, and areas related to the law. Generally, the selections are densely written, use high-level vocabulary, and contain sophisticated argument or complex rhetorical structure (for example, multiple points of view). Reading Comprehension questions require you to read carefully and accurately, to determine the relationships among the various parts of the reading selection, and to draw reasonable inferences from the material in the selection. The questions may ask about the following characteristics of a passage or pair of passages:

- The main idea or primary purpose

- Information that is explicitly stated

- Information or ideas that can be inferred

- The meaning or purpose of words or phrases as used in context

- The organization or structure

- The application of information in the selection to a new context

- Principles that function in the selection

- Analogies to claims or arguments in the selection

- An author's attitude as revealed in the tone of a passage or the language used

- The impact of new information on claims or arguments in the selection

Suggested Approach

Since reading selections are drawn from many different disciplines and sources, you should not be discouraged if you encounter material with which you are not familiar. It is important to remember that questions are to be answered exclusively on the basis of the information provided in the selection. There is no particular knowledge that you are expected to bring to the test, and you should not make inferences based on any prior knowledge of a subject that you may have. You may, however, wish to defer working on a set of questions that seems particularly difficult or unfamiliar until after you have dealt with sets you find easier.

Strategies. One question that often arises in connection with Reading Comprehension has to do with the most effective and efficient order in which to read the selections and questions. Possible approaches include:

- reading the selection very closely and then answering the questions;

- reading the questions first, reading the selection closely, and then returning to the questions; or

- skimming the selection and questions very quickly, then rereading the selection closely and answering the questions.

Test takers are different, and the best strategy for one might not be the best strategy for another. In preparing for the test, therefore, you might want to experiment with the different strategies and decide what works most effectively for you.

Remember that your strategy must be effective under timed conditions. For this reason, the first strategy— reading the selection very closely and then answering the questions—may be the most effective for you. Nonetheless, if you believe that one of the other strategies

might be more effective for you, you should try it out and assess your performance using it.

Reading the selection. Whatever strategy you choose, you should give the passage or pair of passages at least one careful reading before answering the questions. Try to distinguish main ideas from supporting ideas, and opinions or attitudes from factual, objective information. Note transitions from one idea to the next and identify the relationships among the different ideas or parts of a passage, or between the two passages in comparative reading sets. Consider how and why an author makes points and draws conclusions. Be sensitive to implications of what the passages say.

You may find it helpful to mark key parts of passages. For example, you might underline main ideas or important arguments, and you might circle transitional words— "although," "nevertheless," "correspondingly," and the like—that will help you map the structure of a passage. Also, you might note descriptive words that will help you identify an author's attitude toward a particular idea or person.

Answering the Questions

- Always read all the answer choices before selecting the best answer. The best answer choice is the one that most accurately and completely answers the question being posed.

- Respond to the specific question being asked. Do not pick an answer choice simply because it is a true statement. For example, picking a true statement might yield an incorrect answer to a question in which you are asked to identify an author's position on an issue, since you are not being asked to evaluate the truth of the author's position but only to correctly identify what that position is.

- Answer the questions only on the basis of the information provided in the selection. Your own views, interpretations, or opinions, and those you have heard from others, may sometimes conflict with those expressed in a reading selection; however, you are expected to work within the context provided by the reading selection. You should not expect to agree with everything you encounter in reading comprehension passages.

THE WRITING SAMPLE

On the day of the test, you will be asked to write one sample essay. LSAC does not score the writing sample, but copies are sent to all law schools to which you apply. According to a 2006 LSAC survey of 157 United States and Canadian law schools, almost all use the writing sample in evaluating at least some applications for admission. Failure to respond to writing sample prompts and frivolous responses have been used by law schools as grounds for rejection of applications for admission.

In developing and implementing the writing sample portion of the LSAT, LSAC has operated on the following premises: First, law schools and the legal profession value highly the ability to communicate effectively in writing. Second, it is important to encourage potential law students to develop effective writing skills. Third, a sample of an applicant's writing, produced under controlled conditions, is a potentially useful indication of that person's writing ability. Fourth, the writing sample can serve as an independent check on other writing submitted by applicants as part of the admission process. Finally, writing samples may be useful for diagnostic purposes related to improving a candidate's writing.

The writing prompt presents a decision problem. You are asked to make a choice between two positions or courses of action. Both of the choices are defensible, and you are given criteria and facts on which to base your decision. There is no "right" or "wrong" position to take on the topic, so the quality of each test taker's response is a function not of which choice is made, but of how well or poorly the choice is supported and how well or poorly the other choice is criticized.

The LSAT writing prompt was designed and validated by legal education professionals. Since it involves writing based on fact sets and criteria, the writing sample gives applicants the opportunity to demonstrate the type of argumentative writing that is required in law school, although the topics are usually nonlegal.

You will have 35 minutes in which to plan and write an essay on the topic you receive. Read the topic and the accompanying directions carefully. You will probably find it best to spend a few minutes considering the topic and organizing your thoughts before you begin writing. In your essay, be sure to develop your ideas fully, leaving time, if possible, to review what you have written. Do not write on a topic other than the one specified. Writing on a topic of your own choice is not acceptable.

No special knowledge is required or expected for this writing exercise. Law schools are interested in the reasoning, clarity, organization, language usage, and writing mechanics displayed in your essay. How well you write is more important than how much you write. Confine your essay to the blocked, lined area on the front and back of the separate Writing Sample Response Sheet. Only that area will be reproduced for law schools. Be sure that your writing is legible.

TAKING THE PREPTEST UNDER SIMULATED LSAT CONDITIONS

One important way to prepare for the LSAT is to simulate the day of the test by taking a practice test under actual time constraints. Taking a practice test under timed conditions helps you to estimate the amount of time you can afford to spend on each question in a section and to determine the question types on which you may need additional practice.

Since the LSAT is a timed test, it is important to use your allotted time wisely. During the test, you may work only on the section designated by the test supervisor. You can-not devote extra time to a difficult section and make up that time on a section you find easier. In pacing yourself, and checking your answers, you should think of each section of the test as a separate minitest.

Be sure that you answer every question on the test. When you do not know the correct answer to a question, first eliminate the responses that you know are incorrect, then make your best guess among the remaining choices. Do not be afraid to guess as there is no penalty for incorrect answers.

When you take a practice test, abide by all the requirements specified in the directions and keep strictly within the specified time limits. Work without a rest period. When you take an actual test, you will have only a short break—usually 10–15 minutes—after SECTION III.

When taken under conditions as much like actual testing conditions as possible, a practice test provides very useful preparation for taking the LSAT.

Official directions for the four multiple-choice sections and the writing sample are included in this PrepTest so that you can approximate actual testing conditions as you practice.

To take the test:

- Set a timer for 35 minutes. Answer all the questions in SECTION I of this PrepTest. Stop working on that section when the 35 minutes have elapsed.

- Repeat, allowing yourself 35 minutes each for sections II, III, and IV.

- Set the timer again for 35 minutes, then prepare your response to the writing sample topic at the end of this PrepTest.

- Refer to "Computing Your Score" for the PrepTest for instruction on evaluating your performance. An answer key is provided for that purpose.

The practice test that follows consists of four sections corresponding to the four scored sections of the June 2010 LSAT. Also reprinted is the June 2010 unscored writing sample topic.

General Directions for the LSAT Answer Sheet

The actual testing time for this portion of the test will be 2 hours 55 minutes. There are five sections, each with a time limit of 35 minutes. The supervisor will tell you when to begin and end each section. If you finish a section before time is called, you may check your work on that section <u>only</u>; do not turn to any other section of the test book and do not work on any other section either in the test book or on the answer sheet.

There are several different types of questions on the test, and each question type has its own directions. <u>Be sure you understand the directions for each question type before attempting to answer any questions in that section.</u>

Not everyone will finish all the questions in the time allowed. Do not hurry, but work steadily and as quickly as you can without sacrificing accuracy. You are advised to use your time effectively. If a question seems too difficult, go on to the next one and return to the difficult question after completing the section. MARK THE BEST ANSWER YOU CAN FOR EVERY QUESTION. NO DEDUCTIONS WILL BE MADE FOR WRONG ANSWERS. YOUR SCORE WILL BE BASED ONLY ON THE NUMBER OF QUESTIONS YOU ANSWER CORRECTLY.

ALL YOUR ANSWERS MUST BE MARKED ON THE ANSWER SHEET. Answer spaces for each question are lettered to correspond with the letters of the potential answers to each question in the test book. After you have decided which of the answers is correct, blacken the corresponding space on the answer sheet. BE SURE THAT EACH MARK IS BLACK AND COMPLETELY FILLS THE ANSWER SPACE. Give only one answer to each question. If you change an answer, be sure that all previous marks are <u>erased completely</u>. Since the answer sheet is machine scored, incomplete erasures may be interpreted as intended answers. ANSWERS RECORDED IN THE TEST BOOK WILL NOT BE SCORED.

There may be more questions noted on this answer sheet than there are questions in a section. Do not be concerned but be certain that the section and number of the question you are answering matches the answer sheet section and question number. Additional answer spaces in any answer sheet section should be left blank. Begin your next section in the number one answer space for that section.

LSAC takes various steps to ensure that answer sheets are returned from test centers in a timely manner for processing. In the unlikely event that an answer sheet(s) is not received, LSAC will permit the examinee to either retest at no additional fee or to receive a refund of his or her LSAT fee. THESE REMEDIES ARE THE EXCLUSIVE REMEDIES AVAILABLE IN THE UNLIKELY EVENT THAT AN ANSWER SHEET IS NOT RECEIVED BY LSAC.

Score Cancellation

Complete this section only if you are absolutely certain you want to cancel your score. A CANCELLATION REQUEST CANNOT BE RESCINDED. IF YOU ARE AT ALL UNCERTAIN, YOU SHOULD <u>NOT</u> COMPLETE THIS SECTION.

To cancel your score from this administration, you **must:**

A. fill in both ovals here ..... ◯ ◯
          AND

B. read the following statement. Then sign your name and enter the date.
   YOUR SIGNATURE ALONE IS NOT SUFFICIENT FOR SCORE CANCELLATION. BOTH OVALS ABOVE MUST BE FILLED IN FOR SCANNING EQUIPMENT TO RECOGNIZE YOUR REQUEST FOR SCORE CANCELLATION.

I certify that I wish to cancel my test score from this administration. I understand that my request is irreversible and that my score will not be sent to me or to the law schools to which I apply.

_____
Sign your name in full

_____
Date

FOR LSAC USE ONLY ⬤

HOW DID YOU PREPARE FOR THE LSAT?
(Select all that apply.)

Responses to this item are voluntary and will be used for statistical research purposes only.

◯ By studying the free sample questions available on LSAC's website.
◯ By taking the free sample LSAT available on LSAC's website.
◯ By working through official LSAT *PrepTests, ItemWise,* and/or other LSAC test prep products.
◯ By using LSAT prep books or software **not** published by LSAC.
◯ By attending a commercial test preparation or coaching course.
◯ By attending a test preparation or coaching course offered through an undergraduate institution.
◯ Self study.
◯ Other preparation.
◯ No preparation.

CERTIFYING STATEMENT
Please write the following statement. Sign and date.

I certify that I am the examinee whose name appears on this answer sheet and that I am here to take the LSAT for the sole purpose of being considered for admission to law school. I further certify that I will neither assist nor receive assistance from any other candidate, and I agree not to copy or retain examination questions or to transmit them to or discuss them with any other person in any form.

_____
_____
_____
_____
_____
_____
_____
_____
_____

SIGNATURE: _____ TODAY'S DATE: _____/_____/_____
                                                    MONTH DAY YEAR

A

INSTRUCTIONS FOR COMPLETING THE BIOGRAPHICAL AREA ARE ON THE BACK COVER OF YOUR TEST BOOKLET.
USE ONLY A NO. 2 OR HB PENCIL TO COMPLETE THIS ANSWER SHEET. DO NOT USE INK.

USE A NO. 2 OR HB PENCIL ONLY   ● Right Mark   ⊘ ⊗ ⊙ Wrong Marks

1 LAST NAME / FIRST NAME / MI

2 SOCIAL SECURITY / SOCIAL INSURANCE NO.

3 LSAC ACCOUNT NUMBER

L

4 DATE OF BIRTH

MONTH	DAY	YEAR
Jan		
Feb		
Mar		
Apr		
May		
June		
July		
Aug		
Sept		
Oct		
Nov		
Dec		

5 RACIAL/ETHNIC DESCRIPTION
Mark one or more
- 1 Aboriginal/TSI Australian
- 2 Amer. Indian/Alaska Native
- 3 Asian
- 4 Black/African American
- 5 Canadian Aboriginal
- 6 Caucasian/White
- 7 Hispanic/Latino
- 8 Native Hawaiian/ Other Pacific Islander
- 9 Puerto Rican

6 GENDER
- Male
- Female

7 DOMINANT LANGUAGE
- English
- Other

8 ENGLISH FLUENCY
- Yes   - No

9 TEST BOOK SERIAL NO.

10 TEST FORM

11 TEST DATE
MONTH / DAY / YEAR

12 CENTER NUMBER

13 TEST FORM CODE

Law School Admission Test

Mark one and only one answer to each question. Be sure to fill in completely the space for your intended answer choice. If you erase, do so completely. Make no stray marks.

SECTION 1	SECTION 2	SECTION 3	SECTION 4	SECTION 5
1 Ⓐ Ⓑ Ⓒ Ⓓ Ⓔ	1 Ⓐ Ⓑ Ⓒ Ⓓ Ⓔ	1 Ⓐ Ⓑ Ⓒ Ⓓ Ⓔ	1 Ⓐ Ⓑ Ⓒ Ⓓ Ⓔ	1 Ⓐ Ⓑ Ⓒ Ⓓ Ⓔ
2 Ⓐ Ⓑ Ⓒ Ⓓ Ⓔ	2 Ⓐ Ⓑ Ⓒ Ⓓ Ⓔ	2 Ⓐ Ⓑ Ⓒ Ⓓ Ⓔ	2 Ⓐ Ⓑ Ⓒ Ⓓ Ⓔ	2 Ⓐ Ⓑ Ⓒ Ⓓ Ⓔ
3 Ⓐ Ⓑ Ⓒ Ⓓ Ⓔ	3 Ⓐ Ⓑ Ⓒ Ⓓ Ⓔ	3 Ⓐ Ⓑ Ⓒ Ⓓ Ⓔ	3 Ⓐ Ⓑ Ⓒ Ⓓ Ⓔ	3 Ⓐ Ⓑ Ⓒ Ⓓ Ⓔ
4 Ⓐ Ⓑ Ⓒ Ⓓ Ⓔ	4 Ⓐ Ⓑ Ⓒ Ⓓ Ⓔ	4 Ⓐ Ⓑ Ⓒ Ⓓ Ⓔ	4 Ⓐ Ⓑ Ⓒ Ⓓ Ⓔ	4 Ⓐ Ⓑ Ⓒ Ⓓ Ⓔ
5 Ⓐ Ⓑ Ⓒ Ⓓ Ⓔ	5 Ⓐ Ⓑ Ⓒ Ⓓ Ⓔ	5 Ⓐ Ⓑ Ⓒ Ⓓ Ⓔ	5 Ⓐ Ⓑ Ⓒ Ⓓ Ⓔ	5 Ⓐ Ⓑ Ⓒ Ⓓ Ⓔ
6 Ⓐ Ⓑ Ⓒ Ⓓ Ⓔ	6 Ⓐ Ⓑ Ⓒ Ⓓ Ⓔ	6 Ⓐ Ⓑ Ⓒ Ⓓ Ⓔ	6 Ⓐ Ⓑ Ⓒ Ⓓ Ⓔ	6 Ⓐ Ⓑ Ⓒ Ⓓ Ⓔ
7 Ⓐ Ⓑ Ⓒ Ⓓ Ⓔ	7 Ⓐ Ⓑ Ⓒ Ⓓ Ⓔ	7 Ⓐ Ⓑ Ⓒ Ⓓ Ⓔ	7 Ⓐ Ⓑ Ⓒ Ⓓ Ⓔ	7 Ⓐ Ⓑ Ⓒ Ⓓ Ⓔ
8 Ⓐ Ⓑ Ⓒ Ⓓ Ⓔ	8 Ⓐ Ⓑ Ⓒ Ⓓ Ⓔ	8 Ⓐ Ⓑ Ⓒ Ⓓ Ⓔ	8 Ⓐ Ⓑ Ⓒ Ⓓ Ⓔ	8 Ⓐ Ⓑ Ⓒ Ⓓ Ⓔ
9 Ⓐ Ⓑ Ⓒ Ⓓ Ⓔ	9 Ⓐ Ⓑ Ⓒ Ⓓ Ⓔ	9 Ⓐ Ⓑ Ⓒ Ⓓ Ⓔ	9 Ⓐ Ⓑ Ⓒ Ⓓ Ⓔ	9 Ⓐ Ⓑ Ⓒ Ⓓ Ⓔ
10 Ⓐ Ⓑ Ⓒ Ⓓ Ⓔ	10 Ⓐ Ⓑ Ⓒ Ⓓ Ⓔ	10 Ⓐ Ⓑ Ⓒ Ⓓ Ⓔ	10 Ⓐ Ⓑ Ⓒ Ⓓ Ⓔ	10 Ⓐ Ⓑ Ⓒ Ⓓ Ⓔ
11 Ⓐ Ⓑ Ⓒ Ⓓ Ⓔ	11 Ⓐ Ⓑ Ⓒ Ⓓ Ⓔ	11 Ⓐ Ⓑ Ⓒ Ⓓ Ⓔ	11 Ⓐ Ⓑ Ⓒ Ⓓ Ⓔ	11 Ⓐ Ⓑ Ⓒ Ⓓ Ⓔ
12 Ⓐ Ⓑ Ⓒ Ⓓ Ⓔ	12 Ⓐ Ⓑ Ⓒ Ⓓ Ⓔ	12 Ⓐ Ⓑ Ⓒ Ⓓ Ⓔ	12 Ⓐ Ⓑ Ⓒ Ⓓ Ⓔ	12 Ⓐ Ⓑ Ⓒ Ⓓ Ⓔ
13 Ⓐ Ⓑ Ⓒ Ⓓ Ⓔ	13 Ⓐ Ⓑ Ⓒ Ⓓ Ⓔ	13 Ⓐ Ⓑ Ⓒ Ⓓ Ⓔ	13 Ⓐ Ⓑ Ⓒ Ⓓ Ⓔ	13 Ⓐ Ⓑ Ⓒ Ⓓ Ⓔ
14 Ⓐ Ⓑ Ⓒ Ⓓ Ⓔ	14 Ⓐ Ⓑ Ⓒ Ⓓ Ⓔ	14 Ⓐ Ⓑ Ⓒ Ⓓ Ⓔ	14 Ⓐ Ⓑ Ⓒ Ⓓ Ⓔ	14 Ⓐ Ⓑ Ⓒ Ⓓ Ⓔ
15 Ⓐ Ⓑ Ⓒ Ⓓ Ⓔ	15 Ⓐ Ⓑ Ⓒ Ⓓ Ⓔ	15 Ⓐ Ⓑ Ⓒ Ⓓ Ⓔ	15 Ⓐ Ⓑ Ⓒ Ⓓ Ⓔ	15 Ⓐ Ⓑ Ⓒ Ⓓ Ⓔ
16 Ⓐ Ⓑ Ⓒ Ⓓ Ⓔ	16 Ⓐ Ⓑ Ⓒ Ⓓ Ⓔ	16 Ⓐ Ⓑ Ⓒ Ⓓ Ⓔ	16 Ⓐ Ⓑ Ⓒ Ⓓ Ⓔ	16 Ⓐ Ⓑ Ⓒ Ⓓ Ⓔ
17 Ⓐ Ⓑ Ⓒ Ⓓ Ⓔ	17 Ⓐ Ⓑ Ⓒ Ⓓ Ⓔ	17 Ⓐ Ⓑ Ⓒ Ⓓ Ⓔ	17 Ⓐ Ⓑ Ⓒ Ⓓ Ⓔ	17 Ⓐ Ⓑ Ⓒ Ⓓ Ⓔ
18 Ⓐ Ⓑ Ⓒ Ⓓ Ⓔ	18 Ⓐ Ⓑ Ⓒ Ⓓ Ⓔ	18 Ⓐ Ⓑ Ⓒ Ⓓ Ⓔ	18 Ⓐ Ⓑ Ⓒ Ⓓ Ⓔ	18 Ⓐ Ⓑ Ⓒ Ⓓ Ⓔ
19 Ⓐ Ⓑ Ⓒ Ⓓ Ⓔ	19 Ⓐ Ⓑ Ⓒ Ⓓ Ⓔ	19 Ⓐ Ⓑ Ⓒ Ⓓ Ⓔ	19 Ⓐ Ⓑ Ⓒ Ⓓ Ⓔ	19 Ⓐ Ⓑ Ⓒ Ⓓ Ⓔ
20 Ⓐ Ⓑ Ⓒ Ⓓ Ⓔ	20 Ⓐ Ⓑ Ⓒ Ⓓ Ⓔ	20 Ⓐ Ⓑ Ⓒ Ⓓ Ⓔ	20 Ⓐ Ⓑ Ⓒ Ⓓ Ⓔ	20 Ⓐ Ⓑ Ⓒ Ⓓ Ⓔ
21 Ⓐ Ⓑ Ⓒ Ⓓ Ⓔ	21 Ⓐ Ⓑ Ⓒ Ⓓ Ⓔ	21 Ⓐ Ⓑ Ⓒ Ⓓ Ⓔ	21 Ⓐ Ⓑ Ⓒ Ⓓ Ⓔ	21 Ⓐ Ⓑ Ⓒ Ⓓ Ⓔ
22 Ⓐ Ⓑ Ⓒ Ⓓ Ⓔ	22 Ⓐ Ⓑ Ⓒ Ⓓ Ⓔ	22 Ⓐ Ⓑ Ⓒ Ⓓ Ⓔ	22 Ⓐ Ⓑ Ⓒ Ⓓ Ⓔ	22 Ⓐ Ⓑ Ⓒ Ⓓ Ⓔ
23 Ⓐ Ⓑ Ⓒ Ⓓ Ⓔ	23 Ⓐ Ⓑ Ⓒ Ⓓ Ⓔ	23 Ⓐ Ⓑ Ⓒ Ⓓ Ⓔ	23 Ⓐ Ⓑ Ⓒ Ⓓ Ⓔ	23 Ⓐ Ⓑ Ⓒ Ⓓ Ⓔ
24 Ⓐ Ⓑ Ⓒ Ⓓ Ⓔ	24 Ⓐ Ⓑ Ⓒ Ⓓ Ⓔ	24 Ⓐ Ⓑ Ⓒ Ⓓ Ⓔ	24 Ⓐ Ⓑ Ⓒ Ⓓ Ⓔ	24 Ⓐ Ⓑ Ⓒ Ⓓ Ⓔ
25 Ⓐ Ⓑ Ⓒ Ⓓ Ⓔ	25 Ⓐ Ⓑ Ⓒ Ⓓ Ⓔ	25 Ⓐ Ⓑ Ⓒ Ⓓ Ⓔ	25 Ⓐ Ⓑ Ⓒ Ⓓ Ⓔ	25 Ⓐ Ⓑ Ⓒ Ⓓ Ⓔ
26 Ⓐ Ⓑ Ⓒ Ⓓ Ⓔ	26 Ⓐ Ⓑ Ⓒ Ⓓ Ⓔ	26 Ⓐ Ⓑ Ⓒ Ⓓ Ⓔ	26 Ⓐ Ⓑ Ⓒ Ⓓ Ⓔ	26 Ⓐ Ⓑ Ⓒ Ⓓ Ⓔ
27 Ⓐ Ⓑ Ⓒ Ⓓ Ⓔ	27 Ⓐ Ⓑ Ⓒ Ⓓ Ⓔ	27 Ⓐ Ⓑ Ⓒ Ⓓ Ⓔ	27 Ⓐ Ⓑ Ⓒ Ⓓ Ⓔ	27 Ⓐ Ⓑ Ⓒ Ⓓ Ⓔ
28 Ⓐ Ⓑ Ⓒ Ⓓ Ⓔ	28 Ⓐ Ⓑ Ⓒ Ⓓ Ⓔ	28 Ⓐ Ⓑ Ⓒ Ⓓ Ⓔ	28 Ⓐ Ⓑ Ⓒ Ⓓ Ⓔ	28 Ⓐ Ⓑ Ⓒ Ⓓ Ⓔ
29 Ⓐ Ⓑ Ⓒ Ⓓ Ⓔ	29 Ⓐ Ⓑ Ⓒ Ⓓ Ⓔ	29 Ⓐ Ⓑ Ⓒ Ⓓ Ⓔ	29 Ⓐ Ⓑ Ⓒ Ⓓ Ⓔ	29 Ⓐ Ⓑ Ⓒ Ⓓ Ⓔ
30 Ⓐ Ⓑ Ⓒ Ⓓ Ⓔ	30 Ⓐ Ⓑ Ⓒ Ⓓ Ⓔ	30 Ⓐ Ⓑ Ⓒ Ⓓ Ⓔ	30 Ⓐ Ⓑ Ⓒ Ⓓ Ⓔ	30 Ⓐ Ⓑ Ⓒ Ⓓ Ⓔ

14 PLEASE PRINT ALL INFORMATION

LAST NAME   FIRST

SOCIAL SECURITY/SOCIAL INSURANCE NO.

DATE OF BIRTH

MAILING ADDRESS

NOTE: If you have a new address, you must write LSAC at Box 2000-C, Newtown, PA 18940 or call 215.968.1001.

FOR LSAC USE ONLY		
LR	LW	LCS

THE PREPTEST

SECTION I
Time—35 minutes
25 Questions

Directions: The questions in this section are based on the reasoning contained in brief statements or passages. For some questions, more than one of the choices could conceivably answer the question. However, you are to choose the best answer; that is, the response that most accurately and completely answers the question. You should not make assumptions that are by commonsense standards implausible, superfluous, or incompatible with the passage. After you have chosen the best answer, blacken the corresponding space on your answer sheet.

1. Jim's teacher asked him to determine whether a sample of a substance contained iron. Jim knew that magnets attract iron, so he placed a magnet near the substance. Jim concluded that the substance did contain iron, because the substance became attached to the magnet.

   Jim's reasoning is questionable in that it fails to consider the possibility that

   (A) iron sometimes fails to be attracted to magnets
   (B) iron is attracted to other objects besides magnets
   (C) the magnet needed to be oriented in a certain way
   (D) magnets attract substances other than iron
   (E) some magnets attract iron more strongly than others

2. All the books in the library have their proper shelf locations recorded in the catalog. The book Horatio wants is missing from its place on the library shelves, and no one in the library is using it. Since it is not checked out to a borrower nor awaiting shelving nor part of a special display, it must have been either misplaced or stolen.

   Which one of the following most accurately describes the method of reasoning used in the argument?

   (A) An observation about one object is used as a basis for a general conclusion regarding the status of similar objects.
   (B) A deficiency in a system is isolated by arguing that the system failed to control one of the objects that it was intended to control.
   (C) A conclusion about a particular object is rebutted by observing that a generalization that applies to most such objects does not apply to the object in question.
   (D) A generalization is rejected by showing that it fails to hold in one particular instance.
   (E) The conclusion is supported by ruling out other possible explanations of an observed fact.

3. The level of sulfur dioxide in the atmosphere is slightly higher than it was ten years ago. This increase is troubling because ten years ago the Interior Ministry imposed new, stricter regulations on emissions from coal-burning power plants. If these regulations had been followed, then the level of sulfur dioxide in the atmosphere would have decreased.

   Which one of the following can be properly inferred from the statements above?

   (A) If current regulations on emissions from coal-burning power plants are not followed from now on, then the level of sulfur dioxide in the atmosphere will continue to increase.
   (B) There have been violations of the regulations on emissions from coal-burning power plants that were imposed ten years ago.
   (C) If the regulations on emissions from coal-burning power plants are made even stronger, the level of sulfur dioxide in the atmosphere still will not decrease.
   (D) Emissions from coal-burning power plants are one of the main sources of air pollution.
   (E) Government regulations will never reduce the level of sulfur dioxide in the atmosphere.

GO ON TO THE NEXT PAGE.

4. Ecologist: Landfills are generally designed to hold ten years' worth of waste. Some people maintain that as the number of active landfills consequently dwindles over the coming decade, there will inevitably be a crisis in landfill availability. However, their prediction obviously relies on the unlikely assumption that no new landfills will open as currently active ones close and is therefore unsound.

The claim that there will be a crisis in landfill availability plays which one of the following roles in the ecologist's argument?

(A) It follows from the claim stated in the argument's first sentence.
(B) It is the main conclusion of the argument.
(C) It establishes the truth of the argument's conclusion.
(D) It is a claim on which the argument as a whole is designed to cast doubt.
(E) It is an intermediate conclusion of the argument.

5. Recent epidemiological studies report that Country X has the lowest incidence of disease P of any country. Nevertheless, residents of Country X who are reported to have contracted disease P are much more likely to die from it than are residents of any other country.

Which one of the following, if true, most helps to resolve the apparent discrepancy described above?

(A) There are several forms of disease P, some of which are more contagious than others.
(B) Most of the fatal cases of disease P found in Country X involve people who do not reside in Country X.
(C) In Country X, diagnosis of disease P seldom occurs except in the most severe cases of the disease.
(D) The number of cases of disease P that occur in any country fluctuates widely from year to year.
(E) Because of its climate, more potentially fatal illnesses occur in Country X than in many other countries.

6. After an oil spill, rehabilitation centers were set up to save sea otters by removing oil from them. The effort was not worthwhile, however, since 357 affected live otters and 900 that had died were counted, but only 222 affected otters, or 18 percent of those counted, were successfully rehabilitated and survived. Further, the percentage of all those affected that were successfully rehabilitated was much lower still, because only a fifth of the otters that died immediately were ever found.

Which one of the following, as potential challenges, most seriously calls into question evidence offered in support of the conclusion above?

(A) Do sea otters of species other than those represented among the otters counted exist in areas that were not affected by the oil spill?
(B) How is it possible to estimate, of the sea otters that died, how many were not found?
(C) Did the process of capturing sea otters unavoidably involve trapping and releasing some otters that were not affected by the spill?
(D) Were other species of wildlife besides sea otters negatively affected by the oil spill?
(E) What was the eventual cost, per otter rehabilitated, of the rehabilitation operation?

7. Psychologist: Research has shown that a weakened immune system increases vulnerability to cancer. So, cancer-patient support groups, though derided by those who believe that disease is a purely biochemical phenomenon, may indeed have genuine therapeutic value, as it is clear that participation in such groups reduces participants' stress levels.

Which one of the following is an assumption required by the psychologist's argument?

(A) Cancer patients can learn to function well under extreme stress.
(B) Disease is not a biochemical phenomenon at all.
(C) Stress can weaken the immune system.
(D) Discussing one's condition eliminates the stress of being in that condition.
(E) Stress is a symptom of a weakened immune system.

GO ON TO THE NEXT PAGE.

8. Adobe is an ideal material for building in desert environments. It conducts heat very slowly. As a result, a house built of adobe retains the warmth of the desert sun during the cool evenings and then remains cool during the heat of the day, thereby helping to maintain a pleasant temperature. In contrast, houses built of other commonly used building materials, which conduct heat more rapidly, grow hot during the day and cold at night.

Which one of the following most accurately expresses the main conclusion drawn in the argument above?

(A) Adobe is a suitable substitute for other building materials where the heat-conduction properties of the structure are especially important.

(B) In the desert, adobe buildings remain cool during the heat of the day but retain the warmth of the sun during the cool evenings.

(C) Because adobe conducts heat very slowly, adobe houses maintain a pleasant, constant temperature.

(D) Ideally, a material used for building houses in desert environments should enable those houses to maintain a pleasant, constant temperature.

(E) Adobe is an especially suitable material to use for building houses in desert environments.

9. In one study of a particular plant species, 70 percent of the plants studied were reported as having patterned stems. In a second study, which covered approximately the same geographical area, only 40 percent of the plants of that species were reported as having patterned stems.

Which one of the following, if true, most helps to resolve the apparent discrepancy described above?

(A) The first study was carried out at the time of year when plants of the species are at their most populous.

(B) The first study, but not the second study, also collected information about patterned stems in other plant species.

(C) The second study included approximately 15 percent more individual plants than the first study did.

(D) The first study used a broader definition of "patterned."

(E) The focus of the second study was patterned stems, while the first study collected information about patterned stems only as a secondary goal.

10. Letter to the editor: Sites are needed for disposal of contaminated dredge spoils from the local harbor. However, the approach you propose would damage commercial fishing operations. One indication of this is that over 20,000 people have signed petitions opposing your approach and favoring instead the use of sand-capped pits in another area.

Which one of the following most accurately describes a reasoning flaw in the letter's argument?

(A) The argument distorts the editor's view in a manner that makes that view seem more vulnerable to criticism.

(B) The argument fails to establish that the alternative approach referred to is a viable one.

(C) The argument attempts to establish a particular conclusion because doing so is in the letter writer's self-interest rather than because of any genuine concern for the truth of the matter.

(D) The argument's conclusion is based on the testimony of people who have not been shown to have appropriate expertise.

(E) The argument takes for granted that no third option is available that will satisfy all the interested parties.

GO ON TO THE NEXT PAGE.

11. Most universities today offer students a more in-depth and cosmopolitan education than ever before. Until recently, for example, most university history courses required only the reading of textbooks that hardly mentioned the history of Africa or Asia after the ancient periods, or the history of the Americas' indigenous cultures. The history courses at most universities no longer display such limitations.

Which one of the following, if true, most strengthens the argument above?

(A) The history courses that university students find most interesting are comprehensive in their coverage of various periods and cultures.

(B) Many students at universities whose history courses require the reading of books covering all periods and world cultures participate in innovative study-abroad programs.

(C) The extent to which the textbooks of university history courses are culturally inclusive is a strong indication of the extent to which students at those universities get an in-depth and cosmopolitan education.

(D) Universities at which the history courses are quite culturally inclusive do not always have courses in other subject areas that show the same inclusiveness.

(E) University students who in their history courses are required only to read textbooks covering the history of a single culture will not get an in-depth and cosmopolitan education from these courses alone.

12. The government has recently adopted a policy of publishing airline statistics, including statistics about each airline's number of near collisions and its fines for safety violations. However, such disclosure actually undermines the government's goal of making the public more informed about airline safety, because airlines will be much less likely to give complete reports if such information will be made available to the public.

The reasoning in the argument is most vulnerable to criticism on the grounds that it

(A) fails to consider that, even if the reports are incomplete, they may nevertheless provide the public with important information about airline safety

(B) presumes, without providing justification, that the public has a right to all information about matters of public safety

(C) presumes, without providing justification, that information about airline safety is impossible to find in the absence of government disclosures

(D) presumes, without providing justification, that airlines, rather than the government, should be held responsible for accurate reporting of safety information

(E) fails to consider whether the publication of airline safety statistics will have an effect on the revenues of airlines

13. Many economists claim that financial rewards provide the strongest incentive for people to choose one job over another. But in many surveys, most people do not name high salary as the most desirable feature of a job. This shows that these economists overestimate the degree to which people are motivated by money in their job choices.

Which one of the following, if true, most weakens the argument?

(A) Even high wages do not enable people to obtain all the goods they desire.

(B) In many surveys, people say that they would prefer a high-wage job to an otherwise identical job with lower wages.

(C) Jobs that pay the same salary often vary considerably in their other financial benefits.

(D) Many people enjoy the challenge of a difficult job, as long as they feel that their efforts are appreciated.

(E) Some people are not aware that jobs with high salaries typically leave very little time for recreation.

14. Editorial: A proposed new law would limit elementary school class sizes to a maximum of 20 students. Most parents support this measure and argue that making classes smaller allows teachers to devote more time to each student, with the result that students become more engaged in the learning process. However, researchers who conducted a recent study conclude from their results that this reasoning is questionable. The researchers studied schools that had undergone recent reductions in class size, and found that despite an increase in the amount of time teachers spent individually with students, the students' average grades were unchanged.

Which one of the following is an assumption required by the researchers' argument?

(A) The only schools appropriate for study are large elementary schools.

(B) Teachers generally devote the same amount of individualized attention to each student in a class.

(C) Reductions in class size would also involve a decrease in the number of teachers.

(D) Degree of student engagement in the learning process correlates well with students' average grades.

(E) Parental support for the proposed law rests solely on expectations of increased student engagement in the learning process.

GO ON TO THE NEXT PAGE.

15. Camille: Manufacturers of water-saving faucets exaggerate the amount of money such faucets can save. Because the faucets handle such a low volume of water, people using them often let the water run longer than they would otherwise.

Rebecca: It is true that showering now takes longer. Nevertheless, I have had lower water bills since I installed a water-saving faucet. Thus, it is not true that the manufacturers' claims are exaggerated.

The reasoning in Rebecca's argument is questionable in that she takes for granted that

(A) the cost of installing her water-saving faucet was less than her overall savings on her water bill

(B) she saved as much on her water bills as the manufacturers' claims suggested she would

(C) the manufacturers' claims about the savings expected from the installation of water-saving faucets are consistent with one another

(D) people who use water-saving faucets are satisfied with the low volume of water handled by such faucets

(E) installing more water-saving faucets in her house would increase her savings

16. Company spokesperson: In lieu of redesigning our plants, our company recently launched an environmental protection campaign to buy and dispose of old cars, which are generally highly pollutive. Our plants account for just 4 percent of the local air pollution, while automobiles that predate 1980 account for 30 percent. Clearly, we will reduce air pollution more by buying old cars than we would by redesigning our plants.

Which one of the following, if true, most seriously weakens the company spokesperson's argument?

(A) Only 1 percent of the automobiles driven in the local area predate 1980.

(B) It would cost the company over $3 million to reduce its plants' toxic emissions, while its car-buying campaign will save the company money by providing it with reusable scrap metal.

(C) Because the company pays only scrap metal prices for used cars, almost none of the cars sold to the company still run.

(D) Automobiles made after 1980 account for over 30 percent of local air pollution.

(E) Since the company launched its car-buying campaign, the number of citizen groups filing complaints about pollution from the company's plants has decreased.

17. Humankind would not have survived, as it clearly has, if our ancestors had not been motivated by the desire to sacrifice themselves when doing so would ensure the survival of their children or other close relatives. But since even this kind of sacrifice is a form of altruism, it follows that our ancestors were at least partially altruistic.

Which one of the following arguments is most similar in its reasoning to the argument above?

(A) Students do not raise their grades if they do not increase the amount of time they spend studying. Increased study time requires good time management. However, some students do raise their grades. So some students manage their time well.

(B) Organisms are capable of manufacturing their own carbohydrate supply if they do not consume other organisms to obtain it. So plants that consume insects must be incapable of photosynthesis, the means by which most plants produce their carbohydrate supplies.

(C) If fragile ecosystems are not protected by government action their endemic species will perish, for endemic species are by definition those that exist nowhere else but in those ecosystems.

(D) The natural resources used by human beings will be depleted if they are not replaced by alternative materials. But since such replacement generally requires more power, the resources used to create that power will become depleted.

(E) Public buildings do not harmonize with their surroundings if they are not well designed. But any well-designed building is expensive to construct. Thus, either public buildings are expensive to construct or else they do not harmonize with their surroundings.

GO ON TO THE NEXT PAGE.

18. Bus driver: Had the garbage truck not been exceeding the speed limit, it would not have collided with the bus I was driving. I, on the other hand, was abiding by all traffic regulations—as the police report confirms. Therefore, although I might have been able to avoid the collision had I reacted more quickly, the bus company should not reprimand me for the accident.

Which one of the following principles, if valid, most helps to justify the reasoning in the bus driver's argument?

(A) If a vehicle whose driver is violating a traffic regulation collides with a vehicle whose driver is not, the driver of the first vehicle is solely responsible for the accident.

(B) A bus company should not reprimand one of its drivers whose bus is involved in a collision if a police report confirms that the collision was completely the fault of the driver of another vehicle.

(C) Whenever a bus driver causes a collision to occur by violating a traffic regulation, the bus company should reprimand that driver.

(D) A company that employs bus drivers should reprimand those drivers only when they become involved in collisions that they reasonably could have been expected to avoid.

(E) When a bus is involved in a collision, the bus driver should not be reprimanded by the bus company if the collision did not result from the bus driver's violating a traffic regulation.

19. Item Removed From Scoring.

20. Historian: Radio drama requires its listeners to think about what they hear, picturing for themselves such dramatic elements as characters' physical appearances and spatial relationships. Hence, while earlier generations, for whom radio drama was the dominant form of popular entertainment, regularly exercised their imaginations, today's generation of television viewers do so less frequently.

Which one of the following is an assumption required by the historian's argument?

(A) People spend as much time watching television today as people spent listening to radio in radio's heyday.

(B) The more familiar a form of popular entertainment becomes, the less likely its consumers are to exercise their imaginations.

(C) Because it inhibits the development of creativity, television is a particularly undesirable form of popular entertainment.

(D) For today's generation of television viewers, nothing fills the gap left by radio as a medium for exercising the imagination.

(E) Television drama does not require its viewers to think about what they see.

GO ON TO THE NEXT PAGE.

21. Each of the candidates in this year's mayoral election is a small-business owner. Most small-business owners are competent managers. Moreover, no competent manager lacks the skills necessary to be a good mayor. So, most of the candidates in this year's mayoral election have the skills necessary to be a good mayor.

The pattern of flawed reasoning in which one of the following is most similar to that in the argument above?

(A)   Anyone who has worked in sales at this company has done so for at least a year. Most of this company's management has worked in its sales department. So, since no one who has worked in the sales department for more than a year fails to understand marketing, most of this company's upper management understands marketing.

(B)   Everything on the menu at Maddy's Shake Shop is fat-free. Most fat-free foods and drinks are sugar-free. And all sugar-free foods and drinks are low in calories. Hence, most items on the menu at Maddy's are low in calories.

(C)   All the books in Ed's apartment are hardcover books. Most hardcover books are more than 100 pages long. Ed has never read a book longer than 100 pages in its entirety in less than 3 hours. So, Ed has never read any of his books in its entirety in less than 3 hours.

(D)   Each of the avant-garde films at this year's film festival is less than an hour long. Most films less than an hour long do not become commercially successful. So, since no movie less than an hour long has an intermission, it follows that most of the movies at this year's film festival do not have an intermission.

(E)   All of the bicycle helmets sold in this store have some plastic in them. Most of the bicycle helmets sold in this store have some rubber in them. So, since no helmets that have rubber in them do not also have plastic in them, it follows that most of the helmets in this store that have plastic in them have rubber in them.

22. One of the most useful social conventions is money, whose universality across societies is matched only by language. Unlike language, which is rooted in an innate ability, money is an artificial, human invention. Hence, it seems probable that the invention of money occurred independently in more than one society.

The argument's conclusion is properly drawn if which one of the following is assumed?

(A)   Some societies have been geographically isolated enough not to have been influenced by any other society.

(B)   Language emerged independently in different societies at different times in human history.

(C)   Universal features of human society that are not inventions are rooted in innate abilities.

(D)   If money were not useful, it would not be so widespread.

(E)   No human society that adopted the convention of money has since abandoned it.

23. Libel is defined as damaging the reputation of someone by making false statements. Ironically, strong laws against libel can make it impossible for anyone in the public eye to have a good reputation. For the result of strong libel laws is that, for fear of lawsuits, no one will say anything bad about public figures.

Which one of the following principles, if valid, most helps to justify the reasoning in the argument?

(A)   The absence of laws against libel makes it possible for everyone in the public eye to have a good reputation.

(B)   Even if laws against libel are extremely strong and rigorously enforced, some public figures will acquire bad reputations.

(C)   If one makes statements that one sincerely believes, then those statements should not be considered libelous even if they are in fact false and damaging to the reputation of a public figure.

(D)   In countries with strong libel laws, people make negative statements about public figures only when such statements can be proved.

(E)   Public figures can have good reputations only if there are other public figures who have bad reputations.

GO ON TO THE NEXT PAGE.

24. Mammals cannot digest cellulose and therefore cannot directly obtain glucose from wood. Mushrooms can, however; and some mushrooms use cellulose to make highly branched polymers, the branches of which are a form of glucose called beta-glucans. Beta-glucan extracts from various types of mushrooms slow, reverse, or prevent the growth of cancerous tumors in mammals, and the antitumor activity of beta-glucans increases as the degree of branching increases. These extracts prevent tumor growth not by killing cancer cells directly but by increasing immune-cell activity.

Which one of the following is most strongly supported by the information above?

(A) Mammals obtain no beneficial health effects from eating cellulose.
(B) If extracts from a type of mushroom slow, reverse, or prevent the growth of cancerous tumors in mammals, then the mushroom is capable of using cellulose to make beta-glucans.
(C) The greater the degree of branching of beta-glucans, the greater the degree of immune-cell activity it triggers in mammals.
(D) Immune-cell activity in mammals does not prevent tumor growth by killing cancer cells.
(E) Any organism capable of obtaining glucose from wood can use cellulose to make beta-glucans.

25. A law is successful primarily because the behavior it prescribes has attained the status of custom. Just as manners are observed not because of sanctions attached to them but because, through repetition, contrary behavior becomes unthinkable, so societal laws are obeyed not because the behavior is ethically required or because penalties await those who act otherwise, but because to act otherwise would be uncustomary.

Which one of the following comparisons is utilized by the argument?

(A) As with manners and other customs, laws vary from society to society.
(B) As with manners, the primary basis for a society to consider when adopting a law is custom.
(C) As with manners, the main factor accounting for compliance with laws is custom.
(D) As with manners, most laws do not prescribe behavior that is ethically required.
(E) As with manners, most laws do not have strict penalties awaiting those who transgress them.

S T O P

IF YOU FINISH BEFORE TIME IS CALLED, YOU MAY CHECK YOUR WORK ON THIS SECTION ONLY.
DO NOT WORK ON ANY OTHER SECTION IN THE TEST.

SECTION II

Time—35 minutes

23 Questions

<u>Directions:</u> Each group of questions in this section is based on a set of conditions. In answering some of the questions, it may be useful to draw a rough diagram. Choose the response that most accurately and completely answers each question and blacken the corresponding space on your answer sheet.

<u>Questions 1–6</u>

A community center will host six arts-and-crafts workshops—Jewelry, Kite-making, Needlepoint, Quilting, Rug-making, and Scrapbooking. The workshops will be given on three consecutive days: Wednesday, Thursday, and Friday. Each workshop will be given once, and exactly two workshops will be given per day, one in the morning and one in the afternoon. The schedule for the workshops is subject to the following constraints:

　　Jewelry must be given in the morning, on the same day as either Kite-making or Quilting.

　　Rug-making must be given in the afternoon, on the same day as either Needlepoint or Scrapbooking.

　　Quilting must be given on an earlier day than both Kite-making and Needlepoint.

1. Which one of the following is an acceptable schedule for the workshops, with each day's workshops listed in the order in which they are to be given?

　(A)　Wednesday: Jewelry, Kite-making
　　　　Thursday: Quilting, Scrapbooking
　　　　Friday: Needlepoint, Rug-making
　(B)　Wednesday: Jewelry, Quilting
　　　　Thursday: Kite-making, Needlepoint
　　　　Friday: Scrapbooking, Rug-making
　(C)　Wednesday: Quilting, Needlepoint
　　　　Thursday: Scrapbooking, Rug-making
　　　　Friday: Jewelry, Kite-making
　(D)　Wednesday: Quilting, Scrapbooking
　　　　Thursday: Jewelry, Kite-making
　　　　Friday: Rug-making, Needlepoint
　(E)　Wednesday: Scrapbooking, Rug-making
　　　　Thursday: Quilting, Jewelry
　　　　Friday: Kite-making, Needlepoint

2. Which one of the following workshops CANNOT be given on Thursday morning?

　(A)　Jewelry
　(B)　Kite-making
　(C)　Needlepoint
　(D)　Quilting
　(E)　Scrapbooking

3. Which one of the following pairs of workshops CANNOT be the ones given on Wednesday morning and Wednesday afternoon, respectively?

　(A)　Jewelry, Kite-making
　(B)　Jewelry, Quilting
　(C)　Quilting, Scrapbooking
　(D)　Scrapbooking, Quilting
　(E)　Scrapbooking, Rug-making

4. If Kite-making is given on Friday morning, then which one of the following could be true?

　(A)　Jewelry is given on Thursday morning.
　(B)　Needlepoint is given on Thursday afternoon.
　(C)　Quilting is given on Wednesday morning.
　(D)　Rug-making is given on Friday afternoon.
　(E)　Scrapbooking is given on Wednesday afternoon.

5. If Quilting is given in the morning, then which one of the following workshops CANNOT be given on Thursday?

　(A)　Jewelry
　(B)　Kite-making
　(C)　Needlepoint
　(D)　Rug-making
　(E)　Scrapbooking

6. How many of the workshops are there that could be the one given on Wednesday morning?

　(A)　one
　(B)　two
　(C)　three
　(D)　four
　(E)　five

GO ON TO THE NEXT PAGE.

Questions 7–12

Exactly six actors—Geyer, Henson, Jhalani, Lin, Mitchell, and Paredes—will appear one after another in the opening credits of a television program. Their contracts contain certain restrictions that affect the order in which they can appear. Given these restrictions, the order in which the actors appear, from first to sixth, must conform to the following:

  Both Lin and Mitchell appear earlier than Henson.
  Both Lin and Paredes appear earlier than Jhalani.
  If Mitchell appears earlier than Paredes, then Henson appears earlier than Geyer.
  Geyer does not appear last.

7. Which one of the following could be the order, from first to last, in which the actors appear?

  (A) Geyer, Lin, Jhalani, Paredes, Mitchell, Henson
  (B) Geyer, Mitchell, Paredes, Lin, Henson, Jhalani
  (C) Henson, Lin, Paredes, Jhalani, Geyer, Mitchell
  (D) Lin, Paredes, Mitchell, Henson, Jhalani, Geyer
  (E) Paredes, Mitchell, Lin, Jhalani, Geyer, Henson

8. Which one of the following CANNOT be true?

  (A) Henson appears earlier than Geyer.
  (B) Henson appears sixth.
  (C) Lin appears fifth.
  (D) Paredes appears earlier than Mitchell.
  (E) Paredes appears second.

9. Exactly how many of the actors are there any one of whom could appear sixth?

  (A) 5
  (B) 4
  (C) 3
  (D) 2
  (E) 1

10. If Jhalani appears earlier than Mitchell, then which one of the following could be the order in which the other four actors appear, from earliest to latest?

  (A) Geyer, Lin, Paredes, Henson
  (B) Geyer, Paredes, Henson, Lin
  (C) Lin, Henson, Geyer, Paredes
  (D) Lin, Paredes, Henson, Geyer
  (E) Paredes, Lin, Henson, Geyer

11. If Lin appears immediately before Geyer, then which one of the following must be true?

  (A) Geyer appears no later than third.
  (B) Henson appears last.
  (C) Lin appears no later than third.
  (D) Mitchell appears earlier than Geyer.
  (E) Paredes appears first.

12. If Mitchell appears first, then which one of the following must be true?

  (A) Geyer appears fifth.
  (B) Henson appears third.
  (C) Jhalani appears sixth.
  (D) Lin appears second.
  (E) Paredes appears fourth.

GO ON TO THE NEXT PAGE.

Questions 13–17

Over the course of one day, a landscaper will use a truck to haul exactly seven loads—three loads of mulch and four loads of stone. The truck's cargo bed will be cleaned in between carrying any two loads of different materials. To meet the landscaper's needs as efficiently as possible, the following constraints apply:

The cargo bed cannot be cleaned more than three times.
The fifth load must be mulch.

13. Which one of the following is a pair of loads that can both be mulch?

(A) the first and the third
(B) the second and the third
(C) the second and the sixth
(D) the third and the sixth
(E) the fourth and the sixth

14. Which one of the following must be true?

(A) The second load is stone.
(B) The first and second loads are the same material.
(C) The second and third loads are different materials.
(D) At least two loads of mulch are hauled consecutively.
(E) At least three loads of stone are hauled consecutively.

15. If the third load is mulch, which one of the following must be true?

(A) The sixth load is a different material than the seventh load.
(B) The first load is a different material than the second load.
(C) The seventh load is mulch.
(D) The sixth load is mulch.
(E) The first load is stone.

16. If the cargo bed is cleaned exactly twice, which one of the following must be true?

(A) The second load is stone.
(B) The third load is mulch.
(C) The third load is stone.
(D) The sixth load is mulch.
(E) The seventh load is mulch.

17. If no more than two loads of the same material are hauled consecutively, then which one of the following could be true?

(A) The first load is stone.
(B) The fourth load is stone.
(C) The third load is mulch.
(D) The sixth load is mulch.
(E) The seventh load is mulch.

GO ON TO THE NEXT PAGE.

Questions 18–23

A travel magazine has hired six interns—Farber, Gombarick, Hall, Jackson, Kanze, and Lha—to assist in covering three stories—Romania, Spain, and Tuscany. Each intern will be trained either as a photographer's assistant or as a writer's assistant. Each story is assigned a team of two interns—one photographer's assistant and one writer's assistant—in accordance with the following conditions:

Gombarick and Lha will be trained in the same field.
Farber and Kanze will be trained in different fields.
Hall will be trained as a photographer's assistant.
Jackson is assigned to Tuscany.
Kanze is not assigned to Spain.

18. Which one of the following could be an acceptable assignment of photographer's assistants to stories?

(A)   Romania: Farber
        Spain: Hall
        Tuscany: Jackson
(B)   Romania: Gombarick
        Spain: Hall
        Tuscany: Farber
(C)   Romania: Gombarick
        Spain: Hall
        Tuscany: Lha
(D)   Romania: Gombarick
        Spain: Lha
        Tuscany: Kanze
(E)   Romania: Hall
        Spain: Kanze
        Tuscany: Jackson

19. If Farber is assigned to Romania, then which one of the following must be true?

(A)   Gombarick is assigned to Spain.
(B)   Hall is assigned to Spain.
(C)   Kanze is assigned to Tuscany.
(D)   Lha is assigned to Spain.
(E)   Lha is assigned to Tuscany.

20. If Farber and Hall are assigned to the same story as each other, then which one of the following could be true?

(A)   Farber is assigned to Tuscany.
(B)   Gombarick is assigned to Romania.
(C)   Hall is assigned to Romania.
(D)   Kanze is assigned to Tuscany.
(E)   Lha is assigned to Spain.

21. If Farber is a writer's assistant, then which one of the following pairs could be the team of interns assigned to Romania?

(A)   Farber and Gombarick
(B)   Gombarick and Hall
(C)   Hall and Kanze
(D)   Kanze and Lha
(E)   Lha and Hall

22. If Gombarick and Kanze are assigned to the same story as each other, then which one of the following could be true?

(A)   Farber is assigned to Romania.
(B)   Gombarick is assigned to Spain.
(C)   Hall is assigned to Romania.
(D)   Kanze is assigned to Tuscany.
(E)   Lha is assigned to Spain.

23. Which one of the following interns CANNOT be assigned to Tuscany?

(A)   Farber
(B)   Gombarick
(C)   Hall
(D)   Kanze
(E)   Lha

S T O P

IF YOU FINISH BEFORE TIME IS CALLED, YOU MAY CHECK YOUR WORK ON THIS SECTION ONLY.
DO NOT WORK ON ANY OTHER SECTION IN THE TEST.

SECTION III
Time—35 minutes
25 Questions

Directions: The questions in this section are based on the reasoning contained in brief statements or passages. For some questions, more than one of the choices could conceivably answer the question. However, you are to choose the <u>best</u> answer; that is, the response that most accurately and completely answers the question. You should not make assumptions that are by commonsense standards implausible, superfluous, or incompatible with the passage. After you have chosen the best answer, blacken the corresponding space on your answer sheet.

1. A research study revealed that, in most cases, once existing highways near urban areas are widened and extended in an attempt to reduce traffic congestion and resulting delays for motorists, these problems actually increase rather than decrease.

   Which one of the following, if true, most helps to explain the discrepancy between the intended results of the highway improvements and the results revealed in the study?

   (A) Widened and extended roads tend to attract many more motorists than used them before their improvement.

   (B) Typically, road widening or extension projects are undertaken only after the population near the road in question has increased and then leveled off, leaving a higher average population level.

   (C) As a general rule, the greater the number of lanes on a given length of highway, the lower the rate of accidents per 100,000 vehicles traveling on it.

   (D) Rural, as compared to urban, traffic usually includes a larger proportion of trucks and vehicles used by farmers.

   (E) Urban traffic generally moves at a slower pace and involves more congestion and delays than rural and suburban traffic.

2. A study found that consumers reaching supermarket checkout lines within 40 minutes after the airing of an advertisement for a given product over the store's audio system were significantly more likely to purchase the product advertised than were consumers who checked out prior to the airing. Apparently, these advertisements are effective.

   Which one of the following, if true, most strengthens the argument?

   (A) During the study, for most of the advertisements more people went through the checkout lines after they were aired than before they were aired.

   (B) A large proportion of the consumers who bought a product shortly after the airing of an advertisement for it reported that they had not gone to the store intending to buy that product.

   (C) Many of the consumers reported that they typically bought at least one of the advertised products every time they shopped at the store.

   (D) Many of the consumers who bought an advertised product and who reached the checkout line within 40 minutes of the advertisement's airing reported that they could not remember hearing the advertisement.

   (E) Many of the consumers who bought an advertised product reported that they buy that product only occasionally.

GO ON TO THE NEXT PAGE.

3. Unless the building permit is obtained by February 1 of this year or some of the other activities necessary for construction of the new library can be completed in less time than originally planned, the new library will not be completed on schedule. It is now clear that the building permit cannot be obtained by February 1, so the new library will not be completed on schedule.

The conclusion drawn follows logically from the premises if which one of the following is assumed?

(A) All of the other activities necessary for construction of the library will take at least as much time as originally planned.

(B) The officials in charge of construction of the new library have admitted that it probably will not be completed on schedule.

(C) The application for a building permit was submitted on January 2 of this year, and processing building permits always takes at least two months.

(D) The application for a building permit was rejected the first time it was submitted, and it had to be resubmitted with a revised building plan.

(E) It is not possible to convince authorities to allow construction of the library to begin before the building permit is obtained.

4. In a study of patients who enrolled at a sleep clinic because of insomnia, those who inhaled the scent of peppermint before going to bed were more likely to have difficulty falling asleep than were patients who inhaled the scent of bitter orange. Since it is known that inhaling bitter orange does not help people fall asleep more easily, this study shows that inhaling the scent of peppermint makes insomnia worse.

Which one of the following, if true, most seriously weakens the argument above?

(A) Several studies have shown that inhaling the scent of peppermint tends to have a relaxing effect on people who do not suffer from insomnia.

(B) The patients who inhaled the scent of bitter orange were, on average, suffering from milder cases of insomnia than were the patients who inhaled the scent of peppermint.

(C) Because the scents of peppermint and bitter orange are each very distinctive, it was not possible to prevent the patients from knowing that they were undergoing some sort of study of the effects of inhaling various scents.

(D) Some of the patients who enrolled in the sleep clinic also had difficulty staying asleep once they fell asleep.

(E) Several studies have revealed that in many cases inhaling certain pleasant scents can dramatically affect the degree to which a patient suffers from insomnia.

5. Dogs learn best when they are trained using both voice commands and hand signals. After all, a recent study shows that dogs who were trained using both voice commands and hand signals were twice as likely to obey as were dogs who were trained using only voice commands.

The claim that dogs learn best when they are trained using both voice commands and hand signals figures in the argument in which one of the following ways?

(A) It is an explicit premise of the argument.

(B) It is an implicit assumption of the argument.

(C) It is a statement of background information offered to help facilitate understanding the issue in the argument.

(D) It is a statement that the argument claims is supported by the study.

(E) It is an intermediate conclusion that is offered as direct support for the argument's main conclusion.

6. Of the many test pilots who have flown the new plane, none has found it difficult to operate. So it is unlikely that the test pilot flying the plane tomorrow will find it difficult to operate.

The reasoning in which one of the following arguments is most similar to the reasoning in the argument above?

(A) All of the many book reviewers who read Rachel Nguyen's new novel thought that it was particularly well written. So it is likely that the average reader will enjoy the book.

(B) Many of the book reviewers who read Wim Jashka's new novel before it was published found it very entertaining. So it is unlikely that most people who buy the book will find it boring.

(C) Neither of the two reviewers who enjoyed Sharlene Lo's new novel hoped that Lo would write a sequel. So it is unlikely that the review of the book in next Sunday's newspaper will express hope that Lo will write a sequel.

(D) Many reviewers have read Kip Landau's new novel, but none of them enjoyed it. So it is unlikely that the reviewer for the local newspaper will enjoy the book when she reads it.

(E) None of the reviewers who have read Gray Ornsby's new novel were offended by it. So it is unlikely that the book will offend anyone in the general public who reads it.

GO ON TO THE NEXT PAGE.

7. Scientist: Any theory that is to be taken seriously must affect our perception of the world. Of course, this is not, in itself, enough for a theory to be taken seriously. To see this, one need only consider astrology.

    The point of the scientist's mentioning astrology in the argument is to present

    (A) an example of a theory that should not be taken seriously because it does not affect our perception of the world
    (B) an example of something that should not be considered a theory
    (C) an example of a theory that should not be taken seriously despite its affecting our perception of the world
    (D) an example of a theory that affects our perception of the world, and thus should be taken seriously
    (E) an example of a theory that should be taken seriously, even though it does not affect our perception of the world

8. Clark: Our local community theater often produces plays by critically acclaimed playwrights. In fact, the production director says that critical acclaim is one of the main factors considered in the selection of plays to perform. So, since my neighbor Michaela's new play will be performed by the theater this season, she must be a critically acclaimed playwright.

    The reasoning in Clark's argument is most vulnerable to criticism on the grounds that the argument

    (A) takes a condition necessary for a playwright's being critically acclaimed to be a condition sufficient for a playwright's being critically acclaimed
    (B) fails to consider that several different effects may be produced by a single cause
    (C) treats one main factor considered in the selection of plays to perform as though it were a condition that must be met in order for a play to be selected
    (D) uses as evidence a source that there is reason to believe is unreliable
    (E) provides no evidence that a playwright's being critically acclaimed is the result rather than the cause of his or her plays being selected for production

9. Legal theorist: Governments should not be allowed to use the personal diaries of an individual who is the subject of a criminal prosecution as evidence against that individual. A diary is a silent conversation with oneself and there is no relevant difference between speaking to oneself, writing one's thoughts down, and keeping one's thoughts to oneself.

    Which one of the following principles, if valid, provides the most support for the legal theorist's argument?

    (A) Governments should not be allowed to compel corporate officials to surrender interoffice memos to government investigators.
    (B) When crime is a serious problem, governments should be given increased power to investigate and prosecute suspected wrongdoers, and some restrictions on admissible evidence should be relaxed.
    (C) Governments should not be allowed to use an individual's remarks to prosecute the individual for criminal activity unless the remarks were intended for other people.
    (D) Governments should not have the power to confiscate an individual's personal correspondence to use as evidence against the individual in a criminal trial.
    (E) Governments should do everything in their power to investigate and prosecute suspected wrongdoers.

10. A ring of gas emitting X-rays flickering 450 times per second has been observed in a stable orbit around a black hole. In light of certain widely accepted physical theories, that rate of flickering can best be explained if the ring of gas has a radius of 49 kilometers. But the gas ring could not maintain an orbit so close to a black hole unless the black hole was spinning.

    The statements above, if true, most strongly support which one of the following, assuming that the widely accepted physical theories referred to above are correct?

    (A) Black holes that have orbiting rings of gas with radii greater than 49 kilometers are usually stationary.
    (B) Only rings of gas that are in stable orbits around black holes emit flickering X-rays.
    (C) The black hole that is within the ring of gas observed by the astronomers is spinning.
    (D) X-rays emitted by rings of gas orbiting black holes cause those black holes to spin.
    (E) A black hole is stationary only if it is orbited by a ring of gas with a radius of more than 49 kilometers.

GO ON TO THE NEXT PAGE.

11. A mass of "black water" containing noxious organic material swept through Laurel Bay last year. Some scientists believe that this event was a naturally occurring but infrequent phenomenon. The black water completely wiped out five species of coral in the bay, including mounds of coral that were more than two centuries old. Therefore, even if this black water phenomenon has struck the bay before, it did not reach last year's intensity at any time in the past two centuries.

Which one of the following is an assumption required by the argument?

(A) Masses of black water such as that observed last summer come into the bay more frequently than just once every two centuries.

(B) Every species of coral in the bay was seriously harmed by the mass of black water that swept in last year.

(C) The mass of black water that swept through the bay last year did not decimate any plant or animal species that makes use of coral.

(D) The mounds of centuries-old coral that were destroyed were not in especially fragile condition just before the black water swept in last year.

(E) Older specimens of coral in the bay were more vulnerable to damage from the influx of black water than were young specimens.

12. Many nurseries sell fruit trees that they label "miniature." Not all nurseries, however, use this term in the same way. While some nurseries label any nectarine trees of the Stark Sweet Melody variety as "miniature," for example, others do not. One thing that is clear is that if a variety of fruit tree is not suitable for growing in a tub or a pot, no tree of that variety can be correctly labeled "miniature."

Which one of the following can be properly inferred from the information above?

(A) Most nurseries mislabel at least some of their fruit trees.

(B) Some of the nurseries have correctly labeled nectarine trees of the Stark Sweet Melody variety only if the variety is unsuitable for growing in a tub or a pot.

(C) Any nectarine tree of the Stark Sweet Melody variety that a nursery labels "miniature" is labeled incorrectly.

(D) Some nectarine trees that are not labeled "miniature" are labeled incorrectly.

(E) Unless the Stark Sweet Melody variety of nectarine tree is suitable for growing in a tub or a pot, some nurseries mislabel this variety of tree.

13. Psychologist: Identical twins are virtually the same genetically. Moreover, according to some studies, identical twins separated at birth and brought up in vastly different environments show a strong tendency to report similar ethical beliefs, dress in the same way, and have similar careers. Thus, many of our inclinations must be genetic in origin, and not subject to environmental influences.

Which one of the following, if true, would most weaken the psychologist's argument?

(A) Many people, including identical twins, undergo radical changes in their lifestyles at some point in their lives.

(B) While some studies of identical twins separated at birth reveal a high percentage of similar personality traits, they also show a few differences.

(C) Scientists are far from being able to link any specific genes to specific inclinations.

(D) Identical twins who grow up together tend to develop different beliefs, tastes, and careers in order to differentiate themselves from each other.

(E) Twins who are not identical tend to develop different beliefs, tastes, and careers.

14. Human beings can live happily only in a society where love and friendship are the primary motives for actions. Yet economic needs can be satisfied in the absence of this condition, as, for example, in a merchant society where only economic utility motivates action. It is obvious then that human beings _____.

Which one of the following most logically completes the argument?

(A) can live happily only when economic utility is not a motivator in their society

(B) cannot achieve happiness unless their economic needs have already been satisfied

(C) cannot satisfy economic needs by means of interactions with family members and close friends

(D) can satisfy their basic economic needs without obtaining happiness

(E) cannot really be said to have satisfied their economic needs unless they are happy

GO ON TO THE NEXT PAGE.

15. Technologically, it is already possible to produce nonpolluting cars that burn hydrogen rather than gasoline. But the national system of fuel stations that would be needed to provide the hydrogen fuel for such cars does not yet exist. However, this infrastructure is likely to appear and grow rapidly. A century ago no fuel-distribution infrastructure existed for gasoline-powered vehicles, yet it quickly developed in response to consumer demand.

Which one of the following most accurately expresses the conclusion drawn in the argument?

(A) It is already technologically possible to produce nonpolluting cars that burn hydrogen rather than gasoline.

(B) The fuel-distribution infrastructure for hydrogen-powered cars still needs to be created.

(C) If a new kind of technology is developed, the infrastructure needed to support that technology is likely to quickly develop in response to consumer demands.

(D) The fuel-distribution infrastructure for hydrogen-powered cars is likely to appear and grow rapidly.

(E) Hydrogen-powered vehicles will be similar to gasoline-powered vehicles with regard to the amount of consumer demand for their fuel-distribution infrastructure.

16. Wildlife management experts should not interfere with the natural habitats of creatures in the wild, because manipulating the environment to make it easier for an endangered species to survive in a habitat invariably makes it harder for nonendangered species to survive in that habitat.

The argument is most vulnerable to criticism on the grounds that it

(A) fails to consider that wildlife management experts probably know best how to facilitate the survival of an endangered species in a habitat

(B) fails to recognize that a nonendangered species can easily become an endangered species

(C) overlooks the possibility that saving an endangered species in a habitat is incompatible with preserving the overall diversity of species in that habitat

(D) presumes, without providing justification, that the survival of each endangered species is equally important to the health of the environment

(E) takes for granted that preserving a currently endangered species in a habitat does not have higher priority than preserving species in that habitat that are not endangered

17. Any food that is not sterilized and sealed can contain disease-causing bacteria. Once sterilized and properly sealed, however, it contains no bacteria. There are many different acceptable food-preservation techniques; each involves either sterilizing and sealing food or else at least slowing the growth of disease-causing bacteria. Some of the techniques may also destroy natural food enzymes that cause food to spoil or discolor quickly.

If the statements above are true, which one of the following must be true?

(A) All food preserved by an acceptable method is free of disease-causing bacteria.

(B) Preservation methods that destroy enzymes that cause food to spoil do not sterilize the food.

(C) Food preserved by a sterilization method is less likely to discolor quickly than food preserved with other methods.

(D) Any nonsterilized food preserved by an acceptable method can contain disease-causing bacteria.

(E) If a food contains no bacteria, then it has been preserved by an acceptable method.

GO ON TO THE NEXT PAGE.

18. Activities that pose risks to life are acceptable if and only if each person who bears the risks either gains some net benefit that cannot be had without such risks, or bears the risks voluntarily.

Which one of the following judgments most closely conforms to the principle above?

(A) A door-to-door salesperson declines to replace his older car with a new model with more safety features; this is acceptable because the decision not to replace the car is voluntary.

(B) A smoker subjects people to secondhand smoke at an outdoor public meeting; the resulting risks are acceptable because the danger from secondhand smoke is minimal outdoors, where smoke dissipates quickly.

(C) A motorcyclist rides without a helmet; the risk of fatal injury to the motorcyclist thus incurred is acceptable because the motorcyclist incurs this risk willingly.

(D) Motor vehicles are allowed to emit certain low levels of pollution; the resulting health risks are acceptable because all users of motor vehicles share the resulting benefit of inexpensive, convenient travel.

(E) A nation requires all citizens to spend two years in national service; since such service involves no risk to life, the policy is acceptable.

19. Ecologist: One theory attributes the ability of sea butterflies to avoid predation to their appearance, while another attributes this ability to various chemical compounds they produce. Recently we added each of the compounds to food pellets, one compound per pellet. Predators ate the pellets no matter which one of the compounds was present. Thus the compounds the sea butterflies produce are not responsible for their ability to avoid predation.

The reasoning in the ecologist's argument is flawed in that the argument

(A) presumes, without providing justification, that the two theories are incompatible with each other

(B) draws a conclusion about a cause on the basis of nothing more than a statistical correlation

(C) treats a condition sufficient for sea butterflies' ability to avoid predators as a condition required for this ability

(D) infers, from the claim that no individual member of a set has a certain effect, that the set as a whole does not have that effect

(E) draws a conclusion that merely restates material present in one or more of its premises

20. Principle: One should criticize the works or actions of another person only if the criticism will not seriously harm the person criticized and one does so in the hope or expectation of benefiting someone other than oneself.

Application: Jarrett should not have criticized Ostertag's essay in front of the class, since the defects in it were so obvious that pointing them out benefited no one.

Which one of the following, if true, justifies the above application of the principle?

(A) Jarrett knew that the defects in the essay were so obvious that pointing them out would benefit no one.

(B) Jarrett's criticism of the essay would have been to Ostertag's benefit only if Ostertag had been unaware of the defects in the essay at the time.

(C) Jarrett knew that the criticism might antagonize Ostertag.

(D) Jarrett hoped to gain prestige by criticizing Ostertag.

(E) Jarrett did not expect the criticism to be to Ostertag's benefit.

21. Safety consultant: Judged by the number of injuries per licensed vehicle, minivans are the safest vehicles on the road. However, in carefully designed crash tests, minivans show no greater ability to protect their occupants than other vehicles of similar size do. Thus, the reason minivans have such a good safety record is probably not that they are inherently safer than other vehicles, but rather that they are driven primarily by low-risk drivers.

Which one of the following, if true, most strengthens the safety consultant's argument?

(A) When choosing what kind of vehicle to drive, low-risk drivers often select a kind that they know to perform particularly well in crash tests.

(B) Judged by the number of accidents per licensed vehicle, minivans are no safer than most other kinds of vehicles are.

(C) Minivans tend to carry more passengers at any given time than do most other vehicles.

(D) In general, the larger a vehicle is, the greater its ability to protect its occupants.

(E) Minivans generally have worse braking and emergency handling capabilities than other vehicles of similar size.

GO ON TO THE NEXT PAGE.

22. Consumer advocate: There is no doubt that the government is responsible for the increased cost of gasoline, because the government's policies have significantly increased consumer demand for fuel, and as a result of increasing demand, the price of gasoline has risen steadily.

Which one of the following is an assumption required by the consumer advocate's argument?

(A) The government can bear responsibility for that which it indirectly causes.

(B) The government is responsible for some unforeseen consequences of its policies.

(C) Consumer demand for gasoline cannot increase without causing gasoline prices to increase.

(D) The government has an obligation to ensure that demand for fuel does not increase excessively.

(E) If the government pursues policies that do not increase the demand for fuel, gasoline prices tend to remain stable.

23. A species in which mutations frequently occur will develop new evolutionary adaptations in each generation. Since species survive dramatic environmental changes only if they develop new evolutionary adaptations in each generation, a species in which mutations frequently occur will survive dramatic environmental changes.

The flawed pattern of reasoning in which one of the following is most closely parallel to that in the argument above?

(A) In a stone wall that is properly built, every stone supports another stone. Since a wall's being sturdy depends upon its being properly built, only walls that are composed entirely of stones supporting other stones are sturdy.

(B) A play that is performed before a different audience every time will never get the same reaction from any two audiences. Since no plays are performed before the same audience every time, no play ever gets the same reaction from any two audiences.

(C) A person who is perfectly honest will tell the truth in every situation. Since in order to be a morally upright person one must tell the truth at all times, a perfectly honest person will also be a morally upright person.

(D) An herb garden is productive only if the soil that it is planted in is well drained. Since soil that is well drained is good soil, an herb garden is not productive unless it is planted in good soil.

(E) A diet that is healthful is well balanced. Since a well-balanced diet includes fruits and vegetables, one will not be healthy unless one eats fruits and vegetables.

GO ON TO THE NEXT PAGE.

24. Music critic: How well an underground rock group's recordings sell is no mark of that group's success as an underground group. After all, if a recording sells well, it may be because some of the music on the recording is too trendy to be authentically underground; accordingly, many underground musicians consider it desirable for a recording not to sell well. But weak sales may simply be the result of the group's incompetence.

Which one of the following principles, if valid, most helps to justify the music critic's argument?

(A) If an underground rock group is successful as an underground group, its recordings will sell neither especially well nor especially poorly.

(B) An underground rock group is unsuccessful as an underground group if it is incompetent or if any of its music is too trendy to be authentically underground, or both.

(C) Whether an underground group's recordings meet criteria that many underground musicians consider desirable is not a mark of that group's success.

(D) An underground rock group is successful as an underground group if the group is competent but its recordings nonetheless do not sell well.

(E) For an underground rock group, competence and the creation of authentically underground music are not in themselves marks of success.

25. Graham: The defeat of the world's chess champion by a computer shows that any type of human intellectual activity governed by fixed principles can be mastered by machines and thus that a truly intelligent machine will inevitably be devised.

Adelaide: But you are overlooking the fact that the computer in the case you cite was simply an extension of the people who programmed it. It was their successful distillation of the principles of chess that enabled them to defeat a chess champion using a computer.

The statements above provide the most support for holding that Graham and Adelaide disagree about whether

(A) chess is the best example of a human intellectual activity that is governed by fixed principles

(B) chess is a typical example of the sorts of intellectual activities in which human beings characteristically engage

(C) a computer's defeat of a human chess player is an accomplishment that should be attributed to the computer

(D) intelligence can be demonstrated by the performance of an activity in accord with fixed principles

(E) tools can be designed to aid in any human activity that is governed by fixed principles

S T O P

IF YOU FINISH BEFORE TIME IS CALLED, YOU MAY CHECK YOUR WORK ON THIS SECTION ONLY.
DO NOT WORK ON ANY OTHER SECTION IN THE TEST.

SECTION IV
Time—35 minutes
27 Questions

Directions: Each set of questions in this section is based on a single passage or a pair of passages. The questions are to be answered on the basis of what is stated or implied in the passage or pair of passages. For some of the questions, more than one of the choices could conceivably answer the question. However, you are to choose the best answer; that is, the response that most accurately and completely answers the question, and blacken the corresponding space on your answer sheet.

Over the past 50 years, expansive, low-density communities have proliferated at the edges of many cities in the United States and Canada, creating a phenomenon known as suburban sprawl. Andres
(5) Duany, Elizabeth Plater-Zyberk, and Jeff Speck, a group of prominent town planners belonging to a movement called New Urbanism, contend that suburban sprawl contributes to the decline of civic life and civility. For reasons involving the flow of
(10) automobile traffic, they note, zoning laws usually dictate that suburban homes, stores, businesses, and schools be built in separate areas, and this separation robs people of communal space where they can interact and get to know one another. It is as difficult
(15) to imagine the concept of community without a town square or local pub, these town planners contend, as it is to imagine the concept of family independent of the home.

Suburban housing subdivisions, Duany and his
(20) colleagues add, usually contain homes identical not only in appearance but also in price, resulting in a de facto economic segregation of residential neighborhoods. Children growing up in these neighborhoods, whatever their economic
(25) circumstances, are certain to be ill prepared for life in a diverse society. Moreover, because the widely separated suburban homes and businesses are connected only by "collector roads," residents are forced to drive, often in heavy traffic, in order to
(30) perform many daily tasks. Time that would in a town center involve social interaction within a physical public realm is now spent inside the automobile, where people cease to be community members and instead become motorists, competing for road space,
(35) often acting antisocially. Pedestrians rarely act in this manner toward each other. Duany and his colleagues advocate development based on early-twentieth-century urban neighborhoods that mix housing of different prices and offer residents a "gratifying
(40) public realm" that includes narrow, tree-lined streets, parks, corner grocery stores, cafes, small neighborhood schools, all within walking distance. This, they believe, would give people of diverse backgrounds and lifestyles an opportunity to interact
(45) and thus develop mutual respect.

Opponents of New Urbanism claim that migration to sprawling suburbs is an expression of people's legitimate desire to secure the enjoyment and personal mobility provided by the automobile and the
(50) lifestyle that it makes possible. However, the New Urbanists do not question people's right to their own values; instead, they suggest that we should take a more critical view of these values and of the sprawl-

conducive zoning and subdivision policies that reflect
(55) them. New Urbanists are fundamentally concerned with the long-term social costs of the now-prevailing attitude that individual mobility, consumption, and wealth should be valued absolutely, regardless of their impact on community life.

1. Which one of the following most accurately expresses the main point of the passage?

(A) In their critique of policies that promote suburban sprawl, the New Urbanists neglect to consider the interests and values of those who prefer suburban lifestyles.

(B) The New Urbanists hold that suburban sprawl inhibits social interaction among people of diverse economic circumstances, and they advocate specific reforms of zoning laws as a solution to this problem.

(C) The New Urbanists argue that most people find that life in small urban neighborhoods is generally more gratifying than life in a suburban environment.

(D) The New Urbanists hold that suburban sprawl has a corrosive effect on community life, and as an alternative they advocate development modeled on small urban neighborhoods.

(E) The New Urbanists analyze suburban sprawl as a phenomenon that results from short-sighted traffic policies and advocate changes to these traffic policies as a means of reducing the negative effects of sprawl.

2. According to the passage, the New Urbanists cite which one of the following as a detrimental result of the need for people to travel extensively every day by automobile?

(A) It imposes an extra financial burden on the residents of sprawling suburbs, thus detracting from the advantages of suburban life.

(B) It detracts from the amount of time that people could otherwise devote to productive employment.

(C) It increases the amount of time people spend in situations in which antisocial behavior occurs.

(D) It produces significant amounts of air pollution and thus tends to harm the quality of people's lives.

(E) It decreases the amount of time that parents spend in enjoyable interactions with their children.

GO ON TO THE NEXT PAGE.

3. The passage most strongly suggests that the New Urbanists would agree with which one of the following statements?

   (A) The primary factor affecting a neighborhood's conduciveness to the maintenance of civility is the amount of time required to get from one place to another.

   (B) Private citizens in suburbs have little opportunity to influence the long-term effects of zoning policies enacted by public officials.

   (C) People who live in suburban neighborhoods usually have little difficulty finding easily accessible jobs that do not require commuting to urban centers.

   (D) The spatial configuration of suburban neighborhoods both influences and is influenced by the attitudes of those who live in them.

   (E) Although people have a right to their own values, personal values should not affect the ways in which neighborhoods are designed.

4. Which one of the following most accurately describes the author's use of the word "communities" in line 2 and "community" in line 15?

   (A) They are intended to be understood in almost identical ways, the only significant difference being that one is plural and the other is singular.

   (B) The former is intended to refer to dwellings—and their inhabitants—that happen to be clustered together in particular areas; in the latter, the author means that a group of people have a sense of belonging together.

   (C) In the former, the author means that the groups referred to are to be defined in terms of the interests of their members; the latter is intended to refer generically to a group of people who have something else in common.

   (D) The former is intended to refer to groups of people whose members have professional or political ties to one another; the latter is intended to refer to a geographical area in which people live in close proximity to one another.

   (E) In the former, the author means that there are informal personal ties among members of a group of people; the latter is intended to indicate that a group of people have similar backgrounds and lifestyles.

5. Which one of the following, if true, would most weaken the position that the passage attributes to critics of the New Urbanists?

   (A) Most people who spend more time than they would like getting from one daily task to another live in central areas of large cities.

   (B) Most people who often drive long distances for shopping and entertainment live in small towns rather than in suburban areas surrounding large cities.

   (C) Most people who have easy access to shopping and entertainment do not live in suburban areas.

   (D) Most people who choose to live in sprawling suburbs do so because comparable housing in neighborhoods that do not require extensive automobile travel is more expensive.

   (E) Most people who vote in municipal elections do not cast their votes on the basis of candidates' positions on zoning policies.

6. The passage most strongly suggests that which one of the following would occur if new housing subdivisions in suburban communities were built in accordance with the recommendations of Duany and his colleagues?

   (A) The need for zoning laws to help regulate traffic flow would eventually be eliminated.

   (B) There would be a decrease in the percentage of suburban buildings that contain two or more apartments.

   (C) The amount of time that residents of suburbs spend traveling to the central business districts of cities for work and shopping would increase.

   (D) The need for coordination of zoning policies between large-city governments and governments of nearby suburban communities would be eliminated.

   (E) There would be an increase in the per capita number of grocery stores and schools in those suburban communities.

7. The second paragraph most strongly supports the inference that the New Urbanists make which one of the following assumptions?

   (A) Most of those who buy houses in sprawling suburbs do not pay drastically less than they can afford.

   (B) Zoning regulations often cause economically uniform suburbs to become economically diverse.

   (C) City dwellers who do not frequently travel in automobiles often have feelings of hostility toward motorists.

   (D) Few residents of suburbs are aware of the potential health benefits of walking, instead of driving, to carry out daily tasks.

   (E) People generally prefer to live in houses that look very similar to most of the other houses around them.

GO ON TO THE NEXT PAGE.

Passage A

In ancient Greece, Aristotle documented the ability of foraging honeybees to recruit nestmates to a good food source. He did not speculate on how the communication occurred, but he and naturalists since
(5) then have observed that a bee that finds a new food source returns to the nest and "dances" for its nestmates. In the 1940s, von Frisch and colleagues discovered a pattern in the dance. They observed a foraging honeybee's dance, deciphered it, and thereby
(10) deduced the location of the food source the bee had discovered. Yet questions still remained regarding the precise mechanism used to transmit that information.

In the 1960s, Wenner and Esch each discovered independently that dancing honeybees emit low-
(15) frequency sounds, which we now know to come from wing vibrations. Both researchers reasoned that this might explain the bees' ability to communicate effectively even in completely dark nests. But at that time many scientists mistakenly believed that
(20) honeybees lack hearing, so the issue remained unresolved. Wenner subsequently proposed that smell rather than hearing was the key to honeybee communication. He hypothesized that honeybees derive information not from sound, but from odors the
(25) forager conveys from the food source.

Yet Gould has shown that foragers can dispatch bees to sites they had not actually visited, something that would not be possible if odor were in fact necessary to bees' communication. Finally, using a
(30) honeybee robot to simulate the forager's dance, Kirchner and Michelsen showed that sounds emitted during the forager's dance do indeed play an essential role in conveying information about the food's location.

Passage B

(35) All animals communicate in some sense. Bees dance, ants leave trails, some fish emit high-voltage signals. But some species—bees, birds, and primates, for example—communicate symbolically. In an experiment with vervet monkeys in the wild,
(40) Seyfarth, Cheney, and Marler found that prerecorded vervet alarm calls from a loudspeaker elicited the same response as did naturally produced vervet calls alerting the group to the presence of a predator of a particular type. Vervets looked upward upon hearing
(45) an eagle alarm call, and they scanned the ground below in response to a snake alarm call. These responses suggest that each alarm call represents, for vervets, a specific type of predator.

Karl von Frisch was first to crack the code of the
(50) honeybee's dance, which he described as "language." The dance symbolically represents the distance, direction, and quality of newly discovered food. Adrian Wenner and others believed that bees rely on olfactory cues, as well as the dance, to find a food
(55) source, but this has turned out not to be so.

While it is true that bees have a simple nervous system, they do not automatically follow just any information. Biologist James Gould trained foraging

bees to find food in a boat placed in the middle of a
(60) lake and then allowed them to return to the hive to indicate this new location. He found that hive members ignored the foragers' instructions, presumably because no pollinating flowers grow in such a place.

8. The passages have which one of the following aims in common?

(A) arguing that certain nonhuman animals possess human-like intelligence
(B) illustrating the sophistication with which certain primates communicate
(C) describing certain scientific studies concerned with animal communication
(D) airing a scientific controversy over the function of the honeybee's dance
(E) analyzing the conditions a symbolic system must meet in order to be considered a language

9. Which one of the following statements most accurately characterizes a difference between the two passages?

(A) Passage A is concerned solely with honeybee communication, whereas passage B is concerned with other forms of animal communication as well.
(B) Passage A discusses evidence adduced by scientists in support of certain claims, whereas passage B merely presents some of those claims without discussing the support that has been adduced for them.
(C) Passage B is entirely about recent theories of honeybee communication, whereas passage A outlines the historic development of theories of honeybee communication.
(D) Passage B is concerned with explaining the distinction between symbolic and nonsymbolic communication, whereas passage A, though making use of the distinction, does not explain it.
(E) Passage B is concerned with gaining insight into human communication by considering certain types of nonhuman communication, whereas passage A is concerned with these types of nonhuman communication in their own right.

GO ON TO THE NEXT PAGE.

10. Which one of the following statements is most strongly supported by Gould's research, as reported in the two passages?

    (A) When a forager honeybee does not communicate olfactory information to its nestmates, they will often disregard the forager's directions and go to sites of their own choosing.

    (B) Forager honeybees instinctively know where pollinating flowers usually grow and will not dispatch their nestmates to any other places.

    (C) Only experienced forager honeybees are able to locate the best food sources.

    (D) A forager's dances can draw other honeybees to sites that the forager has not visited and can fail to draw other honeybees to sites that the forager has visited.

    (E) Forager honeybees can communicate with their nestmates about a newly discovered food source by leaving a trail from the food source to the honeybee nest.

11. It can be inferred from the passages that the author of passage A and the author of passage B would accept which one of the following statements?

    (A) Honeybees will ignore the instructions conveyed in the forager's dance if they are unable to detect odors from the food source.

    (B) Wenner and Esch established that both sound and odor play a vital role in most honeybee communication.

    (C) Most animal species can communicate symbolically in some form or other.

    (D) The work of von Frisch was instrumental in answering fundamental questions about how honeybees communicate.

    (E) Inexperienced forager honeybees that dance to communicate with other bees in their nest learn the intricacies of the dance from more experienced foragers.

12. Which one of the following most accurately describes a relationship between the two passages?

    (A) Passage A discusses and rejects a position that is put forth in passage B.

    (B) Passage A gives several examples of a phenomenon for which passage B gives only one example.

    (C) Passage A is concerned in its entirety with a phenomenon that passage B discusses in support of a more general thesis.

    (D) Passage A proposes a scientific explanation for a phenomenon that passage B argues cannot be plausibly explained.

    (E) Passage A provides a historical account of the origins of a phenomenon that is the primary concern of passage B.

GO ON TO THE NEXT PAGE.

Most scholars of Mexican American history mark César Chávez's unionizing efforts among Mexican and Mexican American farm laborers in California as the beginning of Chicano political activism in the
(5) 1960s. By 1965, Chávez's United Farm Workers Union gained international recognition by initiating a worldwide boycott of grapes in an effort to get growers in California to sign union contracts. The year 1965 also marks the birth of contemporary
(10) Chicano theater, for that is the year Luis Valdez approached Chávez about using theater to organize farm workers. Valdez and the members of the resulting Teatro Campesino are generally credited by scholars as having initiated the Chicano theater
(15) movement, a movement that would reach its apex in the 1970s.

In the fall of 1965, Valdez gathered a group of striking farm workers and asked them to talk about their working conditions. A former farm worker
(20) himself, Valdez was no stranger to the players in the daily drama that was fieldwork. He asked people to illustrate what happened on the picket lines, and the less timid in the audience delighted in acting out their ridicule of the strikebreakers. Using the farm
(25) workers' basic improvisations, Valdez guided the group toward the creation of what he termed "actos," skits or sketches whose roots scholars have traced to various sources that had influenced Valdez as a student and as a member of the San Francisco Mime
(30) Troupe. Expanding beyond the initial setting of flatbed-truck stages at the fields' edges, the *acto* became the quintessential form of Chicano theater in the 1960s. According to Valdez, the *acto* should suggest a solution to the problems exposed in the
(35) brief comic statement, and, as with any good political theater, it should satirize the opposition and inspire the audience to social action. Because *actos* were based on participants' personal experiences, they had palpable immediacy.
(40) In her book *El Teatro Campesino*, Yolanda Broyles-González rightly criticizes theater historians for having tended to credit Valdez individually with inventing *actos* as a genre, as if the striking farm workers' improvisational talent had depended entirely
(45) on his vision and expertise for the form it took. She traces especially the *actos*' connections to a similar genre of informal, often satirical shows known as *carpas* that were performed in tents to mainly working-class audiences. *Carpas* had flourished
(50) earlier in the twentieth century in the border area of Mexico and the United States. Many participants in the formation of the Teatro no doubt had substantial cultural links to this tradition and likely adapted it to their improvisations. The early development of the
(55) Teatro Campesino was, in fact, a collective accomplishment; still, Valdez's artistic contribution was a crucial one, for the resulting *actos* were neither *carpas* nor theater in the European tradition of Valdez's academic training, but a distinctive genre
(60) with connections to both.

13. Which one of the following most accurately expresses the main point of the passage?

(A) Some theater historians have begun to challenge the once widely accepted view that in creating the Teatro Campesino, Luis Valdez was largely uninfluenced by earlier historical forms.

(B) In crediting Luis Valdez with founding the Chicano theater movement, theater historians have neglected the role of César Chávez in its early development.

(C) Although the creation of the early material of the Teatro Campesino was a collective accomplishment, Luis Valdez's efforts and expertise were essential factors in determining the form it took.

(D) The success of the early Teatro Campesino depended on the special insights and talents of the amateur performers who were recruited by Luis Valdez to participate in creating *actos*.

(E) Although, as Yolanda Broyles-González has pointed out, the Teatro Campesino was a collective endeavor, Luis Valdez's political and academic connections helped bring it recognition.

14. The author uses the word "immediacy" (line 39) most likely in order to express

(A) how little physical distance there was between the performers in the late 1960s *actos* and their audiences

(B) the sense of intimacy created by the performers' technique of addressing many of their lines directly to the audience

(C) the ease with which the Teatro Campesino members were able to develop *actos* based on their own experiences

(D) how closely the director and performers of the Teatro Campesino worked together to build a repertoire of *actos*

(E) how vividly the *actos* conveyed the performers' experiences to their audiences

GO ON TO THE NEXT PAGE.

15. The second sentence of the passage functions primarily in which one of the following ways?

(A) It helps explain both a motivation of those who developed the first *actos* and an important aspect of their subject matter.

(B) It introduces a major obstacle that Valdez had to overcome in gaining public acceptance of the work of the Teatro Campesino.

(C) It anticipates and counters a possible objection to the author's view that the *actos* developed by Teatro Campesino were effective as political theater.

(D) It provides an example of the type of topic on which scholars of Mexican American history have typically focused to the exclusion of theater history.

(E) It helps explain why theater historians, in their discussions of Valdez, have often treated him as though he were individually responsible for inventing *actos* as a genre.

16. The passage indicates that the early *actos* of the Teatro Campesino and the *carpas* were similar in that

(A) both had roots in theater in the European tradition

(B) both were studied by the San Francisco Mime Troupe

(C) both were initially performed on farms

(D) both often involved satire

(E) both were part of union organizing drives

17. It can be inferred from the passage that Valdez most likely held which one of the following views?

(A) As a theatrical model, the *carpas* of the early twentieth century were ill-suited to the type of theater that he and the Teatro Campesino were trying to create.

(B) César Chávez should have done more to support the efforts of the Teatro Campesino to use theater to organize striking farm workers.

(C) Avant-garde theater in the European tradition is largely irrelevant to the theatrical expression of the concerns of a mainly working-class audience.

(D) Actors do not require formal training in order to achieve effective and artistically successful theatrical performances.

(E) The aesthetic aspects of a theatrical work should be evaluated independently of its political ramifications.

18. Based on the passage, it can be concluded that the author and Broyles-González hold essentially the same attitude toward

(A) the influences that shaped *carpas* as a dramatic genre

(B) the motives of theater historians in exaggerating the originality of Valdez

(C) the significance of *carpas* for the development of the genre of the *acto*

(D) the extent of Valdez's acquaintance with *carpas* as a dramatic form

(E) the role of the European tradition in shaping Valdez's contribution to the development of *actos*

19. The information in the passage most strongly supports which one of the following statements regarding the Teatro Campesino?

(A) Its efforts to organize farm workers eventually won the acceptance of a few farm owners in California.

(B) It included among its members a number of individuals who, like Valdez, had previously belonged to the San Francisco Mime Troupe.

(C) It did not play a major role in the earliest efforts of the United Farm Workers Union to achieve international recognition.

(D) Although its first performances were entirely in Spanish, it eventually gave some performances partially in English, for the benefit of non-Spanish-speaking audiences.

(E) Its work drew praise not only from critics in the United States but from critics in Mexico as well.

20. The passage most strongly supports which one of the following?

(A) The *carpas* tradition has been widely discussed and analyzed by both U.S. and Mexican theater historians concerned with theatrical performance styles and methods.

(B) Comedy was a prominent feature of Chicano theater in the 1960s.

(C) In directing the *actos* of the Teatro Campesino, Valdez went to great lengths to simulate or recreate certain aspects of what audiences had experienced in the *carpas*.

(D) Many of the earliest *actos* were based on scripts composed by Valdez, which the farm-worker actors modified to suit their own diverse aesthetic and pragmatic interests.

(E) By the early 1970s, Valdez was using *actos* as the basis for other theatrical endeavors and was no longer directly associated with the Teatro Campesino.

GO ON TO THE NEXT PAGE.

In October 1999, the Law Reform Commission of Western Australia (LRCWA) issued its report, "Review of the Civil and Criminal Justice System." Buried within its 400 pages are several important (5) recommendations for introducing contingency fees for lawyers' services into the state of Western Australia. Contingency-fee agreements call for payment only if the lawyer is successful in the case. Because of the lawyer's risk of financial loss, such charges generally (10) exceed regular fees.

Although there are various types of contingency-fee arrangements, the LRCWA has recommended that only one type be introduced: "uplift" fee arrangements, which in the case of a successful (15) outcome require the client to pay the lawyer's normal fee plus an agreed-upon additional percentage of that fee. This restriction is intended to prevent lawyers from gaining disproportionately from awards of damages and thus to ensure that just compensation to (20) plaintiffs is not eroded. A further measure toward this end is found in the recommendation that contingency-fee agreements should be permitted only in cases where two conditions are satisfied: first, the contingency-fee arrangement must be used only as a (25) last resort when all means of avoiding such an arrangement have been exhausted; and second, the lawyer must be satisfied that the client is financially unable to pay the fee in the event that sufficient damages are not awarded.

(30) Unfortunately, under this recommendation, lawyers wishing to enter into an uplift fee arrangement would be forced to investigate not only the legal issues affecting any proposed litigation, but also the financial circumstances of the potential client (35) and the probable cost of the litigation. This process would likely be onerous for a number of reasons, not least of which is the fact that the final cost of litigation depends in large part on factors that may change as the case unfolds, such as strategies adopted (40) by the opposing side.

In addition to being burdensome for lawyers, the proposal to make contingency-fee agreements available only to the least well-off clients would be unfair to other clients. This restriction would unjustly (45) limit freedom of contract and would, in effect, make certain types of litigation inaccessible to middle-income people or even wealthy people who might not be able to liquidate assets to pay the costs of a trial. More importantly, the primary reasons for entering (50) into contingency-fee agreements hold for all clients. First, they provide financing for the costs of pursuing a legal action. Second, they shift the risk of not recovering those costs, and of not obtaining a damages award that will pay their lawyer's fees, from (55) the client to the lawyer. Finally, given the convergence of the lawyer's interest and the client's interest under a contingency-fee arrangement, it is reasonable to assume that such arrangements increase lawyers' diligence and commitment to their cases.

21. As described in the passage, the uplift fee agreements that the LRCWA's report recommends are most closely analogous to which one of the following arrangements?

(A) People who join together to share the costs of purchasing lottery tickets on a regular basis agree to share any eventual proceeds from a lottery drawing in proportion to the amounts they contributed to tickets purchased for that drawing.

(B) A consulting firm reviews a company's operations. The consulting firm will receive payment only if it can substantially reduce the company's operating expenses, in which case it will be paid double its usual fee.

(C) The returns that accrue from the assumption of a large financial risk by members of a business partnership formed to develop and market a new invention are divided among them in proportion to the amount of financial risk each assumed.

(D) The cost of an insurance policy is determined by reference to the likelihood and magnitude of an eventual loss covered by the insurance policy and the administrative and marketing costs involved in marketing and servicing the insurance policy.

(E) A person purchasing a property receives a loan for the purchase from the seller. In order to reduce risk, the seller requires the buyer to pay for an insurance policy that will pay off the loan if the buyer is unable to do so.

22. The passage states which one of the following?

(A) Contingency-fee agreements serve the purpose of transferring the risk of pursuing a legal action from the client to the lawyer.

(B) Contingency-fee agreements of the kind the LRCWA's report recommends would normally not result in lawyers being paid larger fees than they deserve.

(C) At least some of the recommendations in the LRCWA's report are likely to be incorporated into the legal system in the state of Western Australia.

(D) Allowing contingency-fee agreements of the sort recommended in the LRCWA's report would not affect lawyers' diligence and commitment to their cases.

(E) Usually contingency-fee agreements involve an agreement that the fee the lawyer receives will be an agreed-upon percentage of the client's damages.

GO ON TO THE NEXT PAGE.

23. The author's main purpose in the passage is to

   (A) defend a proposed reform against criticism
   (B) identify the current shortcomings of a legal system and suggest how these should be remedied
   (C) support the view that a recommended change would actually worsen the situation it was intended to improve
   (D) show that a legal system would not be significantly changed if certain proposed reforms were enacted
   (E) explain a suggested reform and critically evaluate it

24. Which one of the following is given by the passage as a reason for the difficulty a lawyer would have in determining whether—according to the LRCWA's recommendations—a prospective client was qualified to enter into an uplift agreement?

   (A) The length of time that a trial may last is difficult to predict in advance.
   (B) Not all prospective clients would wish to reveal detailed information about their financial circumstances.
   (C) Some factors that may affect the cost of litigation can change after the litigation begins.
   (D) Uplift agreements should only be used as a last resort.
   (E) Investigating whether a client is qualified to enter into an uplift agreement would take time away from investigating the legal issues of the case.

25. The phrase "gaining disproportionately from awards of damages" (lines 18–19) is most likely intended by the author to mean

   (A) receiving a payment that is of greater monetary value than the legal services rendered by the lawyer
   (B) receiving a higher portion of the total amount awarded in damages than is reasonable compensation for the professional services rendered and the amount of risk assumed
   (C) receiving a higher proportion of the damages awarded to the client than the client considers fair
   (D) receiving a payment that is higher than the lawyer would have received had the client's case been unsuccessful
   (E) receiving a higher proportion of the damages awarded to the client than the judge or the jury that awarded the damages intended the lawyer to receive

26. According to the passage, the LRCWA's report recommended that contingency-fee agreements

   (A) be used only when it is reasonable to think that such arrangements will increase lawyers' diligence and commitment to their cases
   (B) be used only in cases in which clients are unlikely to be awarded enormous damages
   (C) be used if the lawyer is not certain that the client seeking to file a lawsuit could pay the lawyer's regular fee if the suit were to be unsuccessful
   (D) not be used in cases in which another type of arrangement is practicable
   (E) not be used except in cases where the lawyer is reasonably sure that the client will win damages sufficiently large to cover the lawyer's fees

27. Which one of the following, if true, most seriously undermines the author's criticism of the LRCWA's recommendations concerning contingency-fee agreements?

   (A) The proportion of lawsuits filed by the least well-off litigants tends to be higher in areas where uplift fee arrangements have been widely used than in areas in which uplift agreements have not been used.
   (B) Before the LRCWA's recommendations, lawyers in Western Australia generally made a careful evaluation of prospective clients' financial circumstances before accepting cases that might involve complex or protracted litigation.
   (C) There is strong opposition in Western Australia to any legal reform perceived as favoring lawyers, so it is highly unlikely that the LRCWA's recommendations concerning contingency-fee agreements will be implemented.
   (D) The total fees charged by lawyers who successfully litigate cases under uplift fee arrangements are, on average, only marginally higher than the total fees charged by lawyers who litigate cases without contingency agreements.
   (E) In most jurisdictions in which contingency-fee agreements are allowed, those of the uplift variety are used much less often than are other types of contingency-fee agreements.

S T O P

IF YOU FINISH BEFORE TIME IS CALLED, YOU MAY CHECK YOUR WORK ON THIS SECTION ONLY.
DO NOT WORK ON ANY OTHER SECTION IN THE TEST.

Acknowledgment is made to the following sources from which material has been adapted for use in this test booklet:

Jorge Huerta, "When Sleeping Giants Awaken: Chicano Theatre in the 1960s." ©2002 by The American Society for Theatre Research, Inc.

Jeff Minerd, "Impacts of Sprawl." ©2000 by World Future Society.

GiGi Visscher, "Contingency Fees in Western Australia." ©2000 by eLaw Journal: Murdoch University Electronic Journal of Law. http://www.murdoch.edu.au/elaw/issues/v7n1/visscher71.html.

Wait for the supervisor's instructions before you open the page to the topic.
Please print and sign your name and write the date in the designated spaces below.
Time: 35 Minutes

General Directions

You will have 35 minutes in which to plan and write an essay on the topic inside. Read the topic and the accompanying directions carefully. You will probably find it best to spend a few minutes considering the topic and organizing your thoughts before you begin writing. In your essay, be sure to develop your ideas fully, leaving time, if possible, to review what you have written. **Do not write on a topic other than the one specified. Writing on a topic of your own choice is not acceptable.**

No special knowledge is required or expected for this writing exercise. Law schools are interested in the reasoning, clarity, organization, language usage, and writing mechanics displayed in your essay. How well you write is more important than how much you write.

Confine your essay to the blocked, lined area on the front and back of the separate Writing Sample Response Sheet. Only that area will be reproduced for law schools. Be sure that your writing is legible.

Both this topic sheet and your response sheet must be turned over to the testing staff before you leave the room.

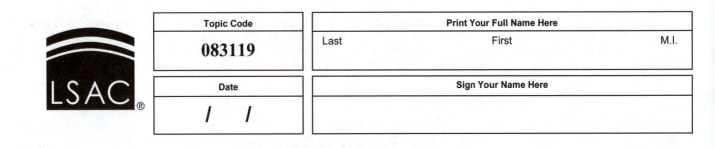

Topic Code	Print Your Full Name Here		
083119	Last	First	M.I.

Date	Sign Your Name Here
/ /	

Scratch Paper
Do not write your essay in this space.

LSAT® Writing Sample Topic

Directions: The scenario presented below describes two choices, either one of which can be supported on the basis of the information given. Your essay should consider both choices and argue for one over the other, based on the two specified criteria and the facts provided. There is no "right" or "wrong" choice: a reasonable argument can be made for either.

In a total solar eclipse, the moon completely covers the sun and casts a rolling shadow along a track on the Earth's surface a few hundred kilometers wide. The eclipse lasts for a few minutes at any location within this track. The Ortegas are planning a trip to observe an upcoming eclipse during their family vacation. They have narrowed the possibilities down to two countries. Using the facts below, write an essay in which you argue in favor of one country over the other based on the following two criteria:

- The Ortegas want to minimize the chance that cloudiness will obscure the eclipse for them.
- The Ortegas want the trip to be worthwhile even if the eclipse is obscured by clouds.

For the first country, climatic data indicate that the probability of cloudiness in the area of the eclipse track is about 75 percent. The family would fly to the capital, which is a cultural center of almost unparalleled richness. Some members of the family have visited the capital before. On some days, they would drive their rental car to other cultural locations in the country. Having a rental car allows some adjustment of eclipse-viewing location according to weather forecasts.

The second country is about twice as far from the family's home as the first country, with correspondingly greater travel expense and inconvenience. No family member has been in the country before. Climatic data indicate that the probability of cloudiness in the area of the eclipse track in the country is about 25 percent. Because the country has some political instability, the family would travel on an eclipse tour organized by a respected company. Visits to several cultural sites are included.

WP-Q083A

Scratch Paper
Do not write your essay in this space.

COMPUTING YOUR SCORE

Directions:

1. Use the Answer Key on the next page to check your answers.

2. Use the Scoring Worksheet below to compute your raw score.

3. Use the Score Conversion Chart to convert your raw score into the 120-180 scale.

Scoring Worksheet

1. Enter the number of questions you answered correctly in each section.

	Number Correct
SECTION I..................	_____
SECTION II.................	_____
SECTION III...............	_____
SECTION IV	_____

2. Enter the sum here: _____
   This is your Raw Score.

Conversion Chart
For Converting Raw Score to the 120-180 LSAT Scaled Score
LSAT Form 1LSN84

Reported Score	Raw Score	
	Lowest	Highest
180	97	99
179	96	96
178	—*	—*
177	95	95
176	94	94
175	93	93
174	92	92
173	91	91
172	90	90
171	89	89
170	87	88
169	86	86
168	85	85
167	83	84
166	82	82
165	80	81
164	79	79
163	77	78
162	75	76
161	74	74
160	72	73
159	70	71
158	68	69
157	67	67
156	65	66
155	63	64
154	62	62
153	60	61
152	58	59
151	56	57
150	55	55
149	53	54
148	51	52
147	50	50
146	48	49
145	47	47
144	45	46
143	43	44
142	42	42
141	40	41
140	39	39
139	37	38
138	36	36
137	35	35
136	33	34
135	32	32
134	31	31
133	29	30
132	28	28
131	27	27
130	26	26
129	25	25
128	24	24
127	23	23
126	22	22
125	21	21
124	20	20
123	19	19
122	18	18
121	17	17
120	0	16

*There is no raw score that will produce this scaled score for this form.

ANSWER KEY

SECTION I

1.	D	8.	E	15.	B	22.	A
2.	E	9.	D	16.	C	23.	E
3.	B	10.	D	17.	A	24.	C
4.	D	11.	C	18.	E	25.	C
5.	C	12.	A	19.	*		
6.	B	13.	C	20.	D		
7.	C	14.	D	21.	B		

SECTION II

1.	B	8.	C	15.	E	22.	E
2.	D	9.	D	16.	A	23.	C
3.	A	10.	A	17.	B		
4.	A	11.	C	18.	A		
5.	E	12.	C	19.	B		
6.	C	13.	E	20.	B		
7.	E	14.	D	21.	D		

SECTION III

1.	A	8.	C	15.	D	22.	A
2.	B	9.	C	16.	E	23.	C
3.	A	10.	C	17.	D	24.	B
4.	B	11.	D	18.	C	25.	C
5.	D	12.	E	19.	D		
6.	D	13.	D	20.	A		
7.	C	14.	D	21.	E		

SECTION IV

1.	D	8.	C	15.	A	22.	A
2.	C	9.	A	16.	D	23.	E
3.	D	10.	D	17.	D	24.	C
4.	B	11.	D	18.	C	25.	B
5.	D	12.	C	19.	C	26.	D
6.	E	13.	C	20.	B	27.	B
7.	A	14.	E	21.	B		

*Item removed from scoring.

LSAT® PREP TOOLS

New! The Official LSAT Handbook

Get to know the LSAT

The LSAT is a test of analytical reasoning, logical reasoning, and reading comprehension, including comparative reading. What's the best way to learn how to approach these types of questions *before* you encounter them on the day of the test? There's no better way than The Official LSAT Handbook, published by the Law School Admission Council, the organization that produces the LSAT. This inexpensive guide will introduce you to the skills that the LSAT is designed to assess so that you can make the most of the rest of your test preparation and do your best on the test. (Note: This handbook contains information that is also included in The Official LSAT SuperPrep. The information in The Official LSAT Handbook has been expanded and updated since it was first published in The Official LSAT SuperPrep.)

$12 ($9.95 online)

LSAC.org